The Art of John Webster

THE ART OF
JOHN
WEBSTER

RALPH BERRY

CLARENDON PRESS · OXFORD

1972

Oxford University Press, Ely House, London W.1

GLASGOW NEW YORK TORONTO MELBOURNE WELLINGTON
CAPE TOWN IBADAN NAIROBI DAR ES SALAAM LUSAKA ADDIS ABABA
DELHI BOMBAY CALCUTTA MADRAS KARACHI LAHORE DACCA
KUALA LUMPUR SINGAPORE HONG KONG TOKYO

PRINTED IN GREAT BRITAIN
BY W & J MACKAY LIMITED CHATHAM

To Mary

PREFACE

THE first decision to make in a book about Webster is whether to attempt a comprehensive study, or to concentrate on certain aspects of his art. Since Clifford Leech's *John Webster* (1951) no one has in fact made the first decision; the large number of scholarly works on Webster of recent years have all been, to a greater or lesser extent, specialized. They are likely to remain so. We now have, through the researches of Gunnar Boklund and R. W. Dent in particular, very full information on Webster's sources and his verbal borrowings. But no definitive work has emerged on Webster as collaborator; and his general indebtedness to his dramatic colleagues has not been properly established, though Travis Bogard and David L. Frost have made important explorations in this field. Until the questions of collaboration and dramatic influences have been thoroughly investigated, the major study of Webster must remain unwritten.

This book has no such ambitious aims. It is confined to the three surviving plays by Webster that are known to be solely his work. I have not sought to study Webster as borrower and source-collector, and I have ignored the Webster of the plays in which he collaborated with other dramatists. It seems to me a sounder enterprise to establish the *echt* Webster of *The White Devil*, *The Duchess of Malfi*, and *The Devil's Law-Case* before turning to the fringe problems of debt and collaboration. For the Webster of these three plays has not, I think, yet been justly weighed. The work of analysis and interpretation still has fresh results and judgements to yield. Hence I have approached Webster through the simple categories of form and content.

The technical characteristics of a Webster play can be usefully approached through the concept of baroque. This stylistic term well describes his dramatic techniques, and indeed draws attention to the most important of them. Webster's plays can thus be seen as attempts to achieve in literature the effects of the baroque, a term which has moreover the advantage of relating Webster to the larger developments in European art.

Content, in a poetic drama, is I believe best apprehended as the themes that the play expresses. But 'theme' is an elusive term. I understand by it an abstraction that can profitably—or at least, persuasively—be derived from a play. One can very reasonably argue, say, that a major theme of *Troilus and Cressida* is the opposition of intuition to reason. Theme is as far as the critic can go in his business of distillation and refinement. But it is not to be thought of as the aim of the dramatist's enterprise. A playwright does not seek to communicate 'themes', of which the plays are vehicles. He depicts a society, or segment of society, involved in certain situations; and the object of the playwright's interest is implied partly in the people, partly in their actions, and partly in their words. This immensely complex event does not, in major drama, yield a neat equation of play to theme. Different critics will dwell, legitimately, on the theme that emerges for them. It is simply a useful way in which the play can be described. I find, then, that I can best write about the content of Webster's plays as a tension between evil and the Law. Clearly, this tension is expressed in much of the explicit subject matter. But above all, it is to be examined in the plays' verbal imagery. This imagery is the most sustained and subtle medium through which Webster's imagination expresses itself.

It does, however, raise the question of the importance that can be assigned to any textual fragment of a Webster play. Here it is helpful to compare Webster with Shakespeare. An image quoted from a Shakespeare play may well be part of a consistent pattern of imagery. But the actual idea, or intellectual point, of the quotation reveals in the first place the character of the speaker, a fact which takes precedence over any other meaning which we may assign to it. Almost the fundamental error of Shakespeare criticism is to extract a given quotation, and embark on an argument which stems essentially from the proposition, 'Shakespeare says . . .' or 'Shakespeare thinks . . .' Now this caution, which of course is relevant in some form to all playwrights, applies less strongly to Webster. He makes, naturally, proper psychological distinctions between his characters. But Webster's dramatis personae seem to draw on a communal hoard of concepts and images, which represent the intellectual substance of his plays. The characters have the double faculty of apparently leading an independent life, while serving as a means whereby their creator passes judgement on them. The range of

ideas and images through which a Websterian character is
allowed to express himself is, in reality, quite narrow, however
complex the ramifications of the scheme may be.
These ideas and image motifs, the substance of the plays, can
properly be analysed in certain broad groups. Webster's plays
are intellectually assembled structures that can be intellectually
dismantled. This process does, however, involve the critic in a
certain weight of quotation. Oddly enough, Webster has I think
been under-quoted in the past. Quotations have tended to present some striking theatrical phrase that has legitimately taken
the fancy of the critic. But the important passages are quite often
not especially striking in themselves; and they are important
because they relate to other passages concerned with the same
idea. I have, accordingly, attempted to strike a balance between a
tedious over-demonstration, and a frail gesture in the direction
of the untold legions of images that can be called up in support
of any central proposition. A ruthless but not inordinate insis-
tence on the existence of parallel passages seems the best target
to aim at. In accordance with my view that the ideas of a Webster
stand more in need of recognition than the poetry and theatrical
effectiveness, I have largely refrained from comment on the
excellences of a given passage. I have, however, relaxed this
policy a little for *The Devil's Law-Case*. It is the most skilful of
his three plays, and much underrated. Webster himself, after
all, thought it fit to be set alongside the two great tragedies.
The Devil's Law-Case is a reduction of the ideas in the tragedies,
and a subtle dramatic essay in its own right. No assessment of
Webster's achievement can succeed without facing up to the
problems it poses.

CONTENTS

LIST OF PLATES

(Between pp. 82–3)

The plates are designed to suggest, rather than supply, a historical frame of reference. Plates 1–4 illustrate the concept of sensationalism, and 5–7 the baroque fascination with illusion and reality. Plates 9–11 are early instances of caricature, and 8 is an advanced grotesque. The baroque artists' awareness of the problems of depicting the human mind is suggested by Plates 12 and 13.

ABBREVIATIONS

Part One

TECHNIQUE

I

INTRODUCTION:
WEBSTER AS BAROQUE ARTIST

WEBSTER is, notoriously, a figure of critical controversy. A recent reviewer has written of the 'extraordinary hostility'[1] that one of his latest censors manifests towards Webster. The phrase, apt enough in its context, could well have been applied to numerous other writers on Webster. How can this hostility be explained? The possible defences enable us to locate the line of the attack. One can say, with Auden, that 'Attacking bad books is not only a waste of time but also bad for the character . . . One cannot attack a bad book without showing off. . . .'[2] This is a comforting assurance that some *mauvais sujets* are to be found among critics hostile to Webster, but does not exclude the possibility that they may be, on occasion, right. Or one can embark on a laboured disputation on each point of the argument; this is tedious, and leads speedily to the conviction that no real dialogue is possible where no language is shared. Between those who see in Webster a morally bankrupt, theatrical trickster (and who take a pious satisfaction in Webster's borrowing, to give it no worse a name) and those who find an ethical coherence reflected in a consistent artistic design, no compromise seems possible. It is clear, as one reads the cries of denunciation that ring out from Canon Kingsley down to the present day, that a central issue is involved. But what is it?

We can give it a name: the myth of decadence. We know no spectacle so ridiculous as the British critical public in one of its periodic fits of morality—as Macaulay might well have said. I cite two instances of the genre, one mid-Victorian, one precisely a century later: *plus ça change*: first, Canon Kingsley:

---

[1] M. A. Shaaber, reviewing Charles O. McDonald's *The Rhetoric of Tragedy* (University of Massachussetts Press, Amherst, Mass., 1966) in *Studies in English Literature 1500–1900*, vii (1967), 355.

[2] W. H. Auden, *The Dyer's Hand* (Faber and Faber, London, 1962), p. 11.

We believe that . . . dramatic art had been steadily growing coarse
from the first years of James; that instead of the arts advancing to per-
fection under Charles I they steadily deteriorated in quality though the
supply became more abundant . . . as the staple interest of the comedies is dirt, so the staple interest in the tragedies is crime. Revenge,
hatred, villainy, incest, and murder upon murder, are their constant
themes and (with the exception of Shakespeare, Ben Jonson in his
earlier plays, and perhaps Massinger) they handle these horrors with
little or no moral purpose, save that of exciting or amusing the audience, and of displaying their own power of delineation in a way which
makes one but too ready to believe the accusations of the Puritans.[3]

Into this scene of decline Webster fits, neatly and predictably:
'The strength of Webster's confest mastership lies simply in his
acquaintance with vicious nature in general. We will say no more
on this matter, save to ask *"Cui bono?"* Was the art of which
this was the highest manifestation likely to be of much use to
mankind?'[4] We can note the intertwined strands of aesthetic and
moral judgement. All critics agree that the plays of the decade
1620–30 are inferior in quality to those of 1610–20; and those
again are inferior to 1600–10. This deterioration is linked, for
the Canon, with the sensationalism of the subject matter and
the plays' lack of moral purpose. Now Mr. L. G. Salingar:
'Webster is sophisticated: but his sophistication belongs to decadence. The poet's solemnity and his groping for a new basis for
tragedy only serve to expose his inner bewilderment and his
lack of any deep sense of communion with his public.'[5] As is usual
with this genre of criticism, 'decadence' is not defined; but one
would still like to know what precisely is meant by it. One must
assume that the sentence that follows does not explain 'decadence'. If it did, one would normally regard 'solemnity and . . .
groping for a new basis for tragedy' as commendably honest
traits in a playwright. The same applies to 'inner bewilderment',
not, one would have thought, so obviously pejorative as Mr.
Salingar assumes. As for 'lack of any deep sense of communion
with his public', one is at a loss to know what to make of this.
Surely this is not to erect box-office success as a valid critical

[3] Charles Kingsley, *Plays and Puritans* (Macmillan, London, 1873), pp. 13,
18–19.
    [4] Ibid., p. 53.
    [5] L. G. Salingar, 'Tourneur and the Tragedy of Revenge', in *The Age of Shake-
speare*, ed. Boris Ford (Penguin, Harmondsworth, 1956), p. 349.

principle? Again, with what portion of his public is Webster deemed to be out of touch? He was well enough thought of by his contemporaries. And can one accept the implicit conclusion that the successful Fletcher—who achieved an all-too-deep *rapport* with his public—is the non-decadent antithesis to the guilty Webster?

The Kingsley-Salingar school of thought points to an attitude that is also, I believe, shared by those who from Archer on have more astutely directed their criticisms towards the technical accomplishment of Webster. That attitude, I suggest, is perfectly comprehensible: it is a simple distaste for the concerns and stylistic traits of the era that Webster represents. Either the critics are neo-classicists (Archer is still the most notable example) in which case Jonson, awkwardly yoked with Shakespeare, is advanced as the model playwright for the times; or they distrust the violence, the emotional excess, the philosophical doubt of the early seventeenth century. The latter attitude finds ready refuge in the myth of decadence; it assumes that a moral decline, of the playwrights and audience, went hand in hand with a decline in quality; though it is not nowadays so foolish as to spell the matter out, it regards the theme of *'Tis Pity She's a Whore* as proof positive of decadence.

Those not under the spell of the myth might, more rationally, conclude that after the achievements of the early seventeenth-century drama nothing other than a decline of sorts could be looked for. No useful critical purpose is served in terming this decline 'decadence' unless the full implications of the term are clearly spelled out. Moreover, even a neutral term such as 'decline' is a generalization that must cover a large number of dramatists. It is not a stick with which to beat any one of them. In this situation, the argument runs: 'X flourishes in a period of decline; therefore X is a decadent; therefore he is, in a rather interesting but unverifiable way, bad.'

Such an argument, plainly, lacks intellectual distinction. Our concern here, however, is with Webster. The true direction for a study of Webster is to see him as he *is*: as a playwright whose methods are the reverse of classical, but which are based on a coherent artistic design. And to comprehend the nature of this design, we have to examine his work without preconceptions as to 'decadence' or 'decline'. A true appraisal of Webster would include an understanding of him in the context of the baroque. To achieve this we must move outside the restricted field of the drama.

It is desirable to view Webster as a part of the main stream of the arts, in Europe, in the early seventeenth century. To this period, beginning roughly in 1600, the art historians have accorded the term baroque. It is generally agreed that baroque art is, in Friedrich's phrase, 'European in scope'.[6] And its usage has spread to other historians, especially of ideas. Nowadays one does not dream of applying the term in a depreciatory, or polemic sense. It is in the first place historically descriptive, and hence neutral in tone. Since Winckelmann's day, historians of art have learned not to regard 'baroque' as synonymous with 'bad taste' and 'error of artistic judgement', together with such adjectives as 'sensational' and 'grotesque' used in a pejorative sense. Nobody is compelled to *like* the baroque style; but it would today be accounted a strange form of *naïveté* to attack it, as a style.

The case of John Webster brings into focus the situation with historians of literature. Too many still tend to be afflicted with a double form of provincialism: an unawareness of the situation in the contemporary arts, and a desire to pass stern judgement upon the style of a man—when it is quite considerably the style of his period—instead of accepting it for what it is. Value judgements of a period masquerade as relative judgements concerning Shakespeare, Middleton, Tourneur, and others of Webster's colleagues. The comparative method has its uses, but it is subject to a caveat: Webster was an extremist. He embodied certain tendencies of his time to a greater extent than any of his contemporaries. But he did this in a strange, and highly individual way. Instead of moving with the *avant-garde*, he produced his great tragedies (in 1612–14) as developments of what the *avant-garde* were writing half a dozen years earlier: the work of Tourneur, Marston, the Shakespeare of *King Lear*. Thence arises the paradox that *The White Devil* and *The Duchess of Malfi* were distinctly old-fashioned at the time of their appearance (Chapman tells us, in 1610, that tragedy was no longer the mode) yet exhibit in extreme form the tendencies of the early baroque era. But this does not affect the main argument. Since style as

<hr />

[6] Carl J. Friedrich, *The Age of the Baroque 1610–1660* (Harper and Row, New York, 1952), p. 39.

such is neutral, anyone wishing to attack a baroque artist is committed to a distinction between 'good' and 'bad' baroque. The present argument seeks to establish first that Webster is a baroque artist, and secondly that he uses its characteristics justifiably.

The main concerns and stylistic traits of the baroque era must now be briefly considered. First, however, a term has to be disposed of: Mannerism. Unlike baroque, Mannerism is still the subject of an art historians' colloquy. It is possible, with Arnold Hauser and Wylie Sypher for example, to regard Mannerism as a descriptive term covering the whole of the period separating the classic Cinquecento from the baroque.[7] Such an approach stresses the tensions, questionings, and dynamism of the period *c.* 1525–*c.* 1600. It regards Tintoretto as a leading example of the Mannerist era. It reaches out to include Shakespeare as a largely Mannerist playwright. But this view is not generally favoured by art historians. For most, Mannerism denotes a style within a period. It is a form of anti-classicism in some (by no means all) Italian painting, sculpture, and architecture from about 1520 to the end of the sixteenth century. This is a virtuoso style, the 'stylish style' (to use Shearman's phrase);[8] poised, sophisticated, exalting art over nature. It is the style of Rosso, Bologna, Parmigianino. Tintoretto is excluded from this concept of Mannerism as too dynamic. The proper literary extension of Mannerism is thus Euphuism; and Shakespeare's relations with Euphuism are one aspect only of his work, whose importance is most obvious in the early part of his career. The matter is by no means stabilized as yet among the art historians, but the reception accorded to John Shearman's authoritative *Mannerism* (1967), the most recent important work of scholarship on the subject, makes it clear that one should adhere to the latter approach. I therefore regard 'Mannerism' as a term that has little or no relevance to the problems of style posed by Webster; and I adopt the customary usage of 'baroque' to describe the period in European artistic development that begins in about 1600.

[7] Arnold Hauser, *The Social Context of Art*, vol. ii: *Renaissance, Mannerism, Baroque* (Routledge and Kegan Paul, London, 1957); Wylie Sypher, *Four Stages of Renaissance Style* (Doubleday, Garden City, New York, 1955).

[8] John Shearman, *Mannerism* (Penguin, Harmondsworth, 1967).

That date is much more than a point of convenience. It signi-
fies, for example, the beginning of *Don Quixote* and quite possi-
bly of *Hamlet*: it is the date of the earliest surviving opera, the
Eurydice of Peri and Caccini, presented at the Pitti Palace in
Florence for the nuptials of Henry IV and Maria de' Medici: it
is the date of the main work of the Carracci, the frescoes in the
Farnese Palace in Rome: it marks the arrival of Rubens, the
great representative of the baroque, at Rome. The year 1600 is in
fact a turning point in the development of the arts, and in thinking about the arts. Tatarkiewicz has shown that around 1600 a
definite shift in aesthetic thinking took place, a move from classical aesthetics to a subjectivist, pluralist, in a word Romantic
aesthetics.[9] Aesthetic values begin the move away from the
object—the repository of beauty—to the spectator.

'Baroque' denotes the inner stylistic unity of the era. It bears
the implication that analogies of subject matter, techniques, and
orientation exist among the arts. Essentially it is an all-
embracing term, and belongs to no one province of histori-
ography. The term was invented and developed by historians of
art, however, and in practice it is proper that it should be used to
draw parallels with the visual arts. For the literary historian, it
offers a methodological opportunity to analyse a work of literature in the categories of a contemporary art. The purpose of this
exercise is twofold. It provides materials for the historian of
ideas, whose function is to synthesize the trends, parallelisms,
the interrelations of ideas in a given period. And the reverse process consolidates the literary historian's judgement of the writer.
To see a writer in isolation, or in relation solely to his literary
colleagues, is to invite two varieties of distortion.

To grant that 'baroque' describes an era is not to ignore
formidable difficulties of analysis. The term, to begin with, is
based on Italian art.[10] Baroque art has in the first place three
historical qualities: it is Italian; it is Roman Catholic; it is im-
bued with the immediate and latent power of the Counter-
Reformation. To assert that baroque is a European phenomenon

[9] W. Tatarkiewicz, 'The Romantic Aesthetics of 1600', *British Journal of
Aesthetics*, vii (1967), 137–49..

[10] 'The whole theory of a Baroque period style must inevitably collapse if the
principle of a derivation of Baroque from the style of the Italian Renaissance is not
maintained.' Helmut Hatzfeld, 'The Baroque from the Viewpoint of the Literary
Historian', *Journal of Aesthetics and Art Criticism*, xiv (1955), 158.

is therefore to make an implicit distinction between original and derived baroque. 'Derived' baroque spreads outwards from Italy: it encounters the perennial classicizing tendencies of the French, the Moorish traditions of Spain, the Protestant structure of England and the United Provinces. At each one of these stages of transmutation, generalizations that apply perfectly to Italian art cease to be appropriate. It is not the purpose of this study to trace the indebtedness of English baroque to Spanish, French, and Italian influences. But one can make allowances for differences of nation, religion, and chronology, and still make generalizations on the stylistic tendencies of the European *avant-garde* in the early seventeenth century.

Perhaps the most useful of these generalizations is provided by Friedrich, who identifies the stylistic characteristics of the period thus: 'Like all styles, it had no uniform set of traits, but can better be described in analogy to two magnetic poles operating within a common field of ideas and feelings. This common field of feeling was focused on movement, intensity, tension, force.'[11] One can add that baroque art, more specifically, exhibits two main areas of interest: the depiction of extreme states of emotion, and the development of naturalism (as a concern of subject matter and of style). It is obsessively concerned with death, and the flux of time. But to make these very reasonable generalizations, one has to concede that they are very far from absolute. The ideas referred to above describe a significant quantity of important work in the baroque era, and distinguish it from the characteristic work of the periods that precede and follow this era. We have then, however, to note the work of the baroque period that is not particularly distinguished by the qualities that have been mentioned.

It is, therefore, an absolute necessity of discourse to acknowledge that baroque art does not exclude expressions of classicism. One can legitimately view the entire history of artistic expression as a sustained dialogue between the classical and anti-classical, a mode that may assume such historical terms as Romantic or baroque. It is clear, most evidently so in France, that classicism was by no means submerged, even temporarily, in the early seventeenth century. One distinguishes, then, between the main line of baroque development—dynamic, emotive, aimed at

11 Friedrich, op. cit., p. 39.

a unified effect—and its classical antithesis, always present, destined to be the dominant mode of the later seventeenth and eighteenth centuries. This mode is less immediately emotive; in the eternal form-content tension, form appears to have gained the upper hand; it is disciplined, tending to formalistic, concerned with the careful articulation of parts. To be sure, baroque as a period term covers all categories. But to employ it usefully—it cannot be a watertight category—one uses it to indicate the qualities of the main line of development. Touchstones for these qualities include Donne, Crashaw, da Cortona, Monteverdi; for classicism, Jonson, Marvell, Annibale Carracci. One can make all manner of further subdivisions of baroque— national, regional, and chronological; Rudolf Wittkower, for example, identifies 'Bolognese late-baroque classicism'. But for my purpose in this study, it is sufficient to identify the qualities of the main line of baroque development. It is these especially that I have in mind when I employ the term. I now consider the major unity that may be discerned in the arts of the baroque era.

The prime concept for understanding baroque art is 'movement'. As first employed by Woelfflin,[12] the word refers strictly to the illusion of motion that baroque architecture conveys. But the other sense of 'move' is more important—that is, the sense that the baroque arts confront the spectator, grapple powerfully with his emotions, and seek masterfully to impose a wide and intense range of sensations upon him. Baroque art is above all sensationalist.

This is evident if one considers the *avant-garde* of the major arts of this period. Music is a leading illustration. Monteverdi, in his Second Practice (that is, a radical break with conventional practice), advances the notion of dissonance; his aim is not to please, in the accepted sense of purveying the accredited harmonies, but to move—and for this, he will widen his whole vocabulary of expression. He seeks to compose music in the *stile concitato*, corresponding to anger, and even undertakes to model music upon a battle. Moreover, it is not only the essence of the three styles of music that appeals to Monteverdi—the *molle*, *concitato*, *temperato*—it is also the sudden transitions from one to

12 H. Woelfflin, *Renaissance and Baroque*, trans. Kathrin Simon (Collins, London, 1964).

another. He makes his brother defend in print his 'mixed modes'.[13] And his *Orfeo* (1607), following the prototype models of a few years earlier, establishes one of the great seventeenth-century art forms, the opera. Gesualdo, again, specializes in the writing of madrigals that are composed expressly to transmit extremes of emotion. His *tempi* vary; the music is frequently impressionistic and unvocal; dissonances are introduced, to coincide with textual references to pain and death. In a word, Gesualdo wishes music to be the servant of the text, hence of the emotions that the texts convey.

Painting shows a parallel tendency towards a wider range of expression, with the clear aim of impressing the spectator. The distortions of El Greco are not, perhaps, the best case in point here, in view of his virtual exile at Toledo; but Caravaggio, at the cross-roads of European painting, serves much better to locate the *avant-garde*. The idea of dissonance finds a ready counterpart in the brusque naturalism of his work. Consider, for example, the entirely naturalistic observation of the tax-gatherers in *The Calling of St. Matthew*, or the bizarre posture in *The Conversion of St. Paul*. Some of Caravaggio's contemporaries thought his work culpably sensationalist, and the charge is worth glancing at here in view of its significance for Webster. There is no question of the sincerity of Caravaggio's religious feelings, and one accepts that this controls his approach to a number of Biblical episodes, like the *St. Matthew*. The sensational is mediated by a reverence for the divine nature of the events. But in some paintings, this is harder to substantiate. The horrific head of *The Beheading of St. John the Baptist* (1607-8) is adequately counterpoised by the brooding, compassionate central figure, and by Salome's spasm of revulsion. (A similar point can be made of *Judith and Holofernes*.) But how of *Medusa*, a shield-painting consisting solely of the face of Medusa caught in the moment of death? This painting is nothing but a depiction of horror; it exists to create a *frisson* in the spectator. We do not need this painting as a justification for Webster's particular development of horror. The instance serves, however, as a reminder that the arts were fascinated with extreme states of

---

[13] See, for example, the foreword to Monteverdi's fifth book of madrigals, reprinted in W. Oliver Strunk, *Source Readings in Music History: The Baroque Era* (Norton, New York, 1965), pp. 45-52.

emotion, and with conveying these states to the spectator. Of the
Beheading, Ellis Waterhouse remarks: 'And the illusion of
space, which not only envelopes the actors but the spectators as
well . . . is almost overpowering. This inducement to the
spectator to participate in the action of the picture is a characteristic of the Roman full Baroque style . . .'[14] A Caravaggio
painting peremptorily demands an audience. The position that he
staked out, an obsession with the brutally realistic aspects of
truth linked with a controlling grasp of design in the expression
of them, is a central one in the movement of the times.

The distinguishing feature of the new poetry is its search for
new metaphors. The search for them is not an end in itself, but a
means of revealing a new truth; and here again the reader is to
be moved, startled. Thus Marino, 'E del poeta il fin la mara-
viglia.' Still more true is this of Donne, whose totally new
extension of metaphorical language marches with an abrasive
manner (and one not simply called forth by the traditional needs
of satire). 'I sing not Siren-like to tempt,/For I am harsh.' The
themes, as in Gryphius and Quevedo, are death, the flux of time,
intense juxtapositions of soul and body. The language matches
the sharp apprehension of mortality. J. M. Cohen has found this
baroque quality most clearly marked in Marino. 'Nothing appears to Marino to have permanent reality.'[15] The baroque poet,
far more than the Renaissance, advances the subjective; the sense
of the uniqueness of the individual's emotions, and that external
events hold primarily the status of metaphors for the individual
mind.

Thus, the major arts show at the turn of the century a new and
radical desire to move, to persuade—if at the risk of alienating
a portion of the public through such shock tactics. It is impossible
to chart the precise interrelations of this European movement:
we can only say that it was in the air, that parallelisms suggest
their own kind of causality. But one important distinction is
necessary here. One type of 'movement' remained at the disposal
of the Roman Catholic Church, expressed itself primarily through
the visual arts, and went on to find its apotheosis in the in-
toxicating debauch of Gaulli's ceiling to the Gesù. That is an

[14] Ellis Waterhouse, *Italian Baroque Painting* (Phaidon, London, 1962), pp.
32–3.
[15] J. M. Cohen, *The Baroque Lyric* (Hutchinson, London, 1963), p. 25.

extreme instance of baroque heightening, of intensified expression. The other type, located in the north of Europe and the Protestant mind, is distinguished by what Rembrandt wrote of as the expression of 'the greatest inward emotion'.[16] This type found its apotheosis in the astonishing portraiture developed in the art of the Netherlands, and in the English drama. It is above all an exploration of naturalism. The moving examination of man, in the interests of truth alone, is the theme of the art we have now to consider.

There are two notable culminations of the general tendencies of baroque. One is the Roman Catholic Church, presenting a *Gesamtkunstwerk* of architecture, painting, music, sculpture, ritual, and incense: its aim is to overwhelm the worshipper with rich sensations, and induce in him a transcendental state of awe. The other is the drama, seeking no less urgently to convince the spectator of the reality it presents. For both, the need to dominate the public is stronger than in any other sphere of public art. Belief, or suspension of disbelief, is the common objective. In England, we have to deal with the second of these phenomena. It is useless to speculate on the notorious English lack of sympathy with the visual arts, but as a matter of historical fact literature and the drama were the only province of the arts that developed rapidly in the early seventeenth century. The factors associated with Continental baroque were absent from the English scene. The English Church was in no position to make the brazen, domineering public gestures of the Roman Catholic Church in Italy and Spain. The Established Church of England was, of doctrinal necessity, no great patron of the iconic arts. The absolutist state of Richelieu, Mazarin, and Louis XIV that supplied the generating force for French baroque found no counterpart in England. The only English government of the seventeenth century that could have expressed its will unequivocally in the arts, as in any other field, was the Protectorate. It built nothing, it closed the stage, it sold Charles I's art collection. The Dutch bourgeoisie, unlike the English, had a tradition and a school of painting that was able to expand very rapidly in response to the favourable social and financial demands of the

---

[16] The exact meaning of the original phrase, 'die meeste ende die naetuereelste beweechgelickheyt', is in some dispute. See Elizabeth G. Holt, *A Documentary History of Art*, ii (Doubleday, Garden City, New York, 1958), 200.

seventeenth century. The historical situation of the English nation, as much perhaps as national genius, pointed away from the full exploration of the baroque style in painting, architecture, and sculpture. It pointed instead to the drama.

The situation of the drama is different from that of the other arts. Here all that is required of the secular power is that it hold the ring; and this, with decreasing difficulty, the Court did until 1642. By the end of the sixteenth century, the assaults of the Puritans upon the stage had been firmly checked. The grand alliance of Court and groundlings had established the stage as the staple of the entertainments industry, and the centre of development in the arts. The way was clear for the creation of a unique blend of talent and genius, brains and money. It is perfectly clear that from the 1590s on drama became *the* modish art. The stage sucked in the talented, the intellectuals, the well born. Nothing is more significant than a comparison of the social origins and standing of Marlowe and Greene with Shakespeare and Webster, and later with Fletcher and Ford. In the years 1590–1610 the social status of the dramatist (and the leading actors) rose amazingly.

The sociology of the baroque does not concern us, however, beyond enabling us to state that in England drama was (with literature) the leading exemplar of the baroque style, and this would still have been true even without the accident of Shakespeare's birth. We have, by 1600, a situation in which the inherent needs of the theatre in all eras coincide with the disposition of the arts generally at that time. The relationship between the baroque and the theatre is, as it were, linguistically established by the very metaphors employed by art historians. Virtually no art historian describes the visual arts of the baroque period without introducing analogies with the theatre. To take two random examples, Eric Newton refers to baroque sculptors working like 'stage designers', and on the same page writes of central European baroque plunging, 'at the slightest provocation into melodrama'.[17] Tapié writes of Bernini's *Cathedra* in St. Peter's, 'Instead of looking at a monument, one finds one is watching a drama . . . But the means employed to realise it

[17] Eric Newton, *European Painting and Sculpture* (Penguin, Harmondsworth, 1941), p. 100.

are none the less theatrical.'[18] If, then, drama is a metaphor for describing the visual arts, one can usefully reverse the process and apply the visual arts as aids to describing, and understanding, the drama.

Primarily, then, the visual arts provide means for the understanding and description of the drama. They point to the inner stylistic unity of the period, but not to overt relations of the sort that we can identify and document. And of the analytic methods for describing the baroque, Woelfflin's categories remain still by far the most important.[19] They offer a way of thinking about the drama, a way which if reasonably pursued can yield valuable insights. But there are two extremes to avoid, and I have sought a middle course between them. At one end is the succession of obvious generalities that everyone agrees on as marks of the baroque. One can assume that few readers would come fresh to the revelation that Webster is obsessed with death and mortality, pre-occupies himself with extreme states of emotions, and is deeply interested in psychology; and that these qualities are especially notable in the baroque era. It is enough for such matters to be glanced at.[20] On the other hand, the over-ingenuity of some critical writing on the interrelationships of the arts can be unsatisfying, if stimulating. There is a perennial danger (when, for example, terms such as 'texture', 'space', 'rhythm' are used outside their appropriate province) that the highly

---

[18] V. L. Tapié, *Age of Grandeur* (Weidenfeld and Nicolson, London, 1960), pp. 55–6.

[19] See H. Woelfflin's *Principles of Art History* (1932), reprinted by Dover Publications, New York, n.d. The five categories enumerated are linear and painterly; plane and recession; closed and open form; multiplicity and unity; clearness and unclearness. A useful discussion of subsequent attempts at formulating Renaissance–Baroque oppositions can be found in Sypher, op. cit., pp. 18–35.

[20] L. L. Schücking, in 'The Baroque Character of the Elizabethan Tragic Hero', *Proceedings of the British Academy*, xxiv (1938), stressed the tendency of the Elizabethan tragic hero to extraordinarily intensified emotional states, and to their expression in extravagant, bizarre language. Schücking's general observations, directed mainly to Shakespeare, have been extended to Marston and Fletcher by Rolf Soellner in 'Baroque Passion in Shakespeare and his Contemporaries', *Shakespeare Studies I*, ed. J. Leeds Barroll (University of Cincinnati Press, Cincinnati, Ohio, 1965), 294–302. Marco Mincoff, in 'Shakespeare, Fletcher, and Baroque Tragedy', *Shakespeare Survey 20* (C.U.P., Cambridge, 1967), ed. Kenneth Muir, 1–15, distinguishes between Shakespearean and Fletcherian tragedy. He sees Fletcher as representing the gateway to seventeenth-century, or Baroque tragedy, with its characteristic love-and-honour conflict. One would doubtless, in this classification, place Webster's tragedies with the Shakespearean type. Still, *The Duchess of Malfi* contains the germ of a love-and-honour play.

metaphorical quality of such terms may weaken their critical usefulness. Analogies of form and technique between arts cannot be pressed too hard. The aim of analogy is persuasion, not demonstration, and I have therefore confined myself to a few central analogies of technique and form.

The basis, then, for the remainder of Part One is this. I regard Webster as a prime, indeed extreme, example of baroque tendencies. It is a corrective to critical judgement to elaborate some of the major parallels that exist between Webster and his contemporaries, especially in the visual arts. The search for these parallels has the double function of illuminating certain methods of Webster, and of anchoring him more firmly than has yet been appreciated to the dominant movement of his times. First, I examine some of the implications of sensationalism, a quality which is fundamental to the baroque and must be accepted as fundamental to Webster's art. Next, I consider the intellectual accompaniment of sensationalism, irony, especially its variant, parody—a form that parallels caricature. Portrait and character-study provide a very obvious field of comparison, and I believe that the Woelfflin category of *malerisch* (painterly) can be applied without violence. Finally, the Woelfflin principle of multiplicity and unity finds its counterpart in the structure of the Webster play, a close-knit texture of imagery, theme, plot, and character.

II

SENSATIONALISM AND MOVEMENT

THE baroque objective of moving the spectator finds a ready medium in the theatre. For obvious reasons, the theatre goes beyond the other arts in its need to dominate the reactions of its audience. It exists by virtue of its power to affect the emotions of its audience, and do so on a regular and commercially sound basis. It is a tense and demanding relationship with the public. So sensationalism, in the broadest sense, is found in all theatres and all ages. But in the English theatre of the early seventeenth century, certain historical intensifying factors can be traced. The influence of Seneca; the very broadly based audience, ensuring that the theatre would not be a coterie affair;[21] the national reluctance of the English to accept conventions not endorsed by empirical need; the honest supply-and-demand capitalism that fostered the rapid growth of the theatre industry; last—and without wrong last to be named, as Webster would say—the sheer sensationalism of contemporary life, to which drama was reputed to hold a mirror—all created a theatre which specialized in working strongly upon the emotions of the audience. And it has frequently been criticized, in the pursuit of the sensational, for an excessive and at times perverted concern with horror, violence and the more recondite modes of sex.

The charge is worth examining, since it bears especially upon Webster. Certainly the Elizabethan drama early became fixed in a pattern wherein acts of the most grotesque horror were presented on stage. It is not clear that in this respect the Jacobean stage had anything to learn from *The Spanish Tragedy* onwards, which culminates in the moving (and presumably redundant) line: 'Lo, see where Hieronymo hath bitten forth his tongue.' From 1589 on, therefore, case law had established that

---

[21] For an analysis of that audience, see especially Alfred Harbage's *Shakespeare's Audience* (Columbia University Press, New York, 1941), pp. 53–91.

on the stage virtually anything goes.[22] A parallel concern with violence and horror is observable in the contemporary arts. The (to us) harmless Monteverdi conveyed, to a conservative contemporary, a brutal obsession with war and horror. Caravaggio's *The Flagellation* (1606–7) finely illustrates his blend of pity and terror. (The painting is largely in darkness, a quality imitated by his Neapolitan following, the 'Tenebrists'. 'Tenebrist' would be a good term for Webster.) The analogue to the blinding of Gloucester in *King Lear* is Rembrandt's *The Blinding of Samson* (1636); and this is even less endurable, for on stage the business can be performed so that the audience cannot see it properly, whereas Rembrandt confronts us with the actual face of the maimed Samson, the limbs writhing in agony. The light-dark symbolism is in Rembrandt too, but combined with a physical realism that surpasses Shakespeare's. The Italian and Spanish painters especially found, in the Crucifixion, a sufficient theme for the depiction of extreme anguish and pathos; on occasion it is perfectly plain that their interest in the Crucifixion as a religious event is decidedly secondary. The considerable number of baroque paintings of Salome and John the Baptist, and Judith and Holofernes, is in itself a significant fact. And naturally the two great sado-erotic favourites of painters, *The Rape of the Sabine Women* and *The Massacre of the Innocents*, offered a perennial invitation to the sensational.

On general and historical grounds, therefore, it should be quite unnecessary to defend Webster against the charge of sensationalism in his plays. The question then becomes: where does the baroque desire to *move* degenerate into mechanical, and culpable, production of sensation? One has to distinguish between means and ends, and relate the sensational event to the pattern of the play. So we can justify the killing of Edward II as an obscene but artistically legitimate comment on his vice; and the blinding of Gloucester as a necessary embodiment of the play's theme of seeing and blindness. In such instances the charge that sensationalism becomes an end in itself can be refuted without too much difficulty.

When we consider Webster's major work, *The White Devil*

[22] M. C. Bradbrook notes the tendency of Elizabethan productions to extract the utmost realism out of scenes of violence and torture. See *Themes and Conventions of Elizabethan Tragedy* (C.U.P., Cambridge, 1935), pp. 18–19, 23.

offers no particular problem. The genre is that of *The Revenger's Tragedy* (1606) and *The Malcontent* (1603); it is a burlesque morality, poised between tragedy and tragi-comedy. Its theme is reward and punishment, appropriate to comedy as well as tragedy; its style, audacious excess. Stylistically, the norm is provided by Flamineo's fake suicide. The genre is not Grand Guignol, and its concerns are those of tragedy; but it does not adopt the tragic mode whole-heartedly. It requires to be played with aplomb and daring, and should cultivate some—but not too many—laughs. The 1966–7 revival of *The Revenger's Tragedy* at the Royal Shakespeare Theatre, Stratford-upon-Avon, demonstrated perfectly how the genre should be played. The fall of Vindice (as of Flamineo) is, at the end, tragic, and meant to be so received by the audience; but it follows a series of episodes that are witty, outrageous, and sensational. Into this pattern and style the events of *The White Devil* fit readily. Camillo's death on a vaulting horse is a legitimate *frisson*, given the genre; Brachiano's poisoning is a dramatically appropriate requital for the poisoning of Isabella; the black humour of the unction-bringing Franciscans (a pun, of course) is wickedly effective; the killings are standard; the ghost is not, perhaps, a good idea, but it is a part of the tradition; Flamineo's outrageous parody of death is, quite simply, funny—he delivers a ham performance of death, bellowing about the plumber laying pipes in his guts—then, quite suddenly, the real thing is upon him, and the audience. The laughter stops. The tone changes. The grotesquerie, the calculated excess, the *Galgenhumor* have almost convinced us that it is not so. But it is so. Nothing can be the same again, in the work of an artist who does not repeat himself. *The Duchess of Malfi* begins, as it ends, in the terrible conviction that it *is* so.

The Duchess of Malfi is a quite different sort of play, It is a tragedy. It discards the style of excess, that is to say, of the mode that denies through exaggeration. The horrors of a great many dramatic representations would be unendurable, could not the mind take refuge in the assurance: 'it is not so; it is too exaggerated to be true.' On such pretexts, the mind seizes very readily. But the horrors of *The Duchess of Malfi* are of a quite different order. They are excessive, because they represent a very great quantum of human pain. They do not proffer an obvious excuse for rejection. Webster takes his action very seriously throughout the play, and means his audience to do likewise.

It is *The Duchess of Malfi* that has drawn the fire of the critics. The prolonged horrors of the fourth act, ever since Lamb's misjudged praise, have been the usual target. Archer's phrases still astonish: the work of 'a morbid-minded schoolboy . . . A grisly monstrosity . . .' Again: 'The wax works . . . are a monstrous improbability . . .'[23] This should not nowadays be worth refuting, but since it is still advanced,[24] it still merits rebuttal. L. G. Salingar phrases the charge thus: 'His paraphernalia of revenge and torture are neither purely sensational nor emblems of poetic justice, but are presented with an effort at naturalism, and with the aim of exciting nervous horror and foreboding. . . .'[25] If the torture was 'purely sensational', would this be relative praise ? And if it is not 'purely sensational', why has it 'the aim of exciting nervous horror and foreboding' ? And why should the reference to 'poetic justice' be introduced, since it does not apply to the Duchess, and even in literary criticism there are limits to the usefulness of saying what something is not ? Let us clarify the matter. The primary purpose of the waxworks and the dead hand is not to horrify us; it is to horrify the Duchess. The fourth act is about the prolonged mental torture of the Duchess; her reactions are what constitute the drama. It is the Duchess, not the audience, who is tortured; the audience is moved, less by the waxworks, than by their effect on the Duchess.[26] The quotations do not begin to formulate a serious charge.

Nevertheless, the waxworks issue raises some points of dramatic aesthetics that should be glanced at. Suppose that in a given production of *The Duchess of Malfi* (original, or modern) the waxen images of death are so presented as to create the maximum effect upon the audience, as well as on the Duchess. This is a matter of theatre on which one cannot generalize, since it can only be judged in its immediate context. But the

---

[23] W. Archer, *The Old Drama and the New* (Dodd, Mead, Boston, Mass., 1924), p. 57.

[24] Ian Jack, 'The Case of John Webster', *Scrutiny*, xvi (1949), 38–43.

[25] L. G. Salingar, op. cit., p. 349.

[26] A comparable distinction can be made of Middleton's *The Changeling*, III. iv. 27–32 (New Mermaid edition). The horror of the situation lies not in the severed finger, but that Beatrice finds it horrible—she who had commissioned the murder.

aesthetic principles involved ought to be established. Wax-works, as it happens, have come to be identified with a harmless form of induced horror. If, however, we can project our thought back in time through the Tussaud barrier, we can see that a waxwork body is merely a *simulacrum* of death and violence; no more, no less. I do not perceive the distinction between wax-works and other paraphernalia of stage violence—the actors' blood, the property heads, and the rest of the *matériel* catalogued in Henslowe's diary, much of it perfectly relevant to the stage today. Nor can I see that a stage deception embodied in a property item (e.g. a severed hand) is more reprehensible than one com-municated through the actor's make-up, as in the empty sockets of Gloucester. Accept one device, accept all. The problem can be posed more brutally: what is the aesthetic distinction be-tween a live actor simulating a corpse on the stage, and a waxen image of the same corpse? One might say, the 'dead' actor is a necessity of stagecraft, hence allowable; whereas the waxworks are a fake even in the play context. But in Act IV of *The Duchess of Malfi* Antonio is still alive, consequently his corpse can only be represented in counterfeit. Naturally one requires that this be convincingly staged; but this, one gathers, is not what the anti-waxwork critics maintain; they denounce waxworks *per se*. The difficulty is that the whole of the theatre is a vast mechanism for inducing effects, some of its expedients being highly ingenious. To distinguish between the legitimate and illegitimate expedient is hardly possible within the realm of theory. Unless, then, as a dramatic fundamentalist one is prepared to ban all spectacle, all mechanical aids to the actor (an attitude of singular purity) I cannot see how these problems may be resolved. In sum, the argument against waxworks as a theatrical means appears thin. And this is true even before one reaches for arguments justifying the Websterian waxworks on quite different grounds, based on the symbolic meaning of the *simulacra* of death. The waxworks embody the appearance-reality theme, they figure mortality, and they suggestively parallel Cariola's comment on the Duchess's appearance,

> Like to your picture in the gallery,
> A deal of life in shew, but none in practise:
>
> (IV. ii. 33–4)[27]

27 All quotations from Webster are from *The Complete Works of John Webster,*

At all events, the critical argument hereabouts is not one that can be settled by invoking the shade of Madame Tussaud.

The Duchess of Malfi should be studied as a play strongly influenced by *King Lear*: and the Duchess's

> Th'heaven ore my head, seemes made of molten brasse,
> The earth of flaming sulphure, yet I am not mad:
>
> (IV. ii. 27–8)

parallels Lear's

> I am bound
> Upon a wheel of fire, that mine own tears
> Do scald like molten lead.
>
> (IV. vii. 46–8)

The major climax of the action, the ordeal of the Duchess, is presented not only in action but through images. Here we need to scrutinize Webster's sensationalism much more closely; the verbal images of bodily sensation throw a particularly clear light on Webster's methods. One has only to review the evidence to realize at once that here is no haphazard collection of individually effective sayings. One will look in vain among these images for sensations of pleasure, vitality, and health. Pain and feverishness stamp themselves upon the bodily sensations projected in this play.

The sensation of a fever is an alternation between extremes of heat and cold. We find this idea frequently embodied in the imagery. Thus Ferdinand:

> had I bin damn'd in hell,
> And should have heard of this, it would have put me
> Into a cold sweat:
>
> (II. v. 97–9)

Antonio:

> 'Tis ev'n like him, that in a winter night
> Takes a long slumber, ore a dying fire:
> As loth to part from't; yet parts thence as cold,
> As when he first sat downe.
>
> (III. ii. 237–40)

---

ed. F. L. Lucas, 4 vols. (Chatto and Windus, London, 1927). This edition, together with its editorial commentary, is designated as 'Lucas'.

This image echoes his earlier

> But he's a foole
> That (being a-cold) would thrust his hands i'th'fire
> To warme them.
>
> (I. i. 489-91)

Particularly this cold touches Bosola. He speaks of his intelligence 'freezing' (II. iii. 6): says 'I'll not freeze i'th'businesse' (v. ii. 147): and states clearly the fever sensation, 'We seeme to sweate in yce, and freeze in fire' (IV. ii. 364). Further hints come from the Duchess, who speaks of freezing to death (IV. i. 79-80): yet, in a later passage,

> Th'heaven ore my head, seemes made of molten brasse,
> The earth of flaming sulphure . . .
>
> (IV. ii. 27-8)

The Doctor brings Ferdinand

> a Salamanders skin, to keepe you
> From sun-burning.
>
> (v. ii. 60-1)

Extremes of cold and heat; is there an image that combines these sensations? The question need only be asked, to receive an immediate answer: the ague.
Thrice Webster employs this metaphor:

> *Ferdinand.* Intemperate agues, make Physitians cruell.
>
> (IV. i. 170)
>
> *Antonio.* I'll be out of this Ague;
>
> (v. iii. 59)

And, most important of all—the words are dying—

> *Antonio.* Pleasure of life, what is't? onely the good houres
> Of an Ague:
>
> (v. iv. 78-9)

This last saying is often quoted as an example of Webster's verbal brilliance, and of his profoundly pessimistic outlook. It is more than that. The ague image gathers to itself the sensations of heat and cold that are scattered elsewhere in the play. And images of pain, even torture, mingle with those of fever. The Duchess's wooing presents the idea; she speaks of making her will now, rather

Then in deepe groanes, and terrible ghastly lookes,
As if the guifts we parted with, procur'd
That violent distraction . . .

(i. i. 430–2)

Later we have images of the bee-sting (iv. i. 93–4): two of the
toothache (iv. ii. 156, and v. v. 78–80): and 'cruell sore eyes'
(v. ii. 62). Ferdinand speaks of a stream of gall through his
heart (iv. ii. 305–6): his brother, as Julia reports, of a

piteous wound i'th'heart,
And a sicke livour . . .

(ii. iv. 48–9)

These images support the general idea of sickness and disease.
But other pain images directly refer to the torture chamber:

Cardinal. Doe not put thy selfe
To such a voluntary torture:

(ii. iv. 12–13)

Duchess. Good comfortable fellow
Perswade a wretch that's broke upon the wheele
To have all his bones new set: entreate him live,
To be executed again:

(iv. i. 95–8)

Cardinal. Will you rack me?

(v. ii. 265)

Such images find their direct embodiment in the fourth act, the
systematic mental torture of the Duchess. Plainly, the devices of
the waxworks and dead hand stand not merely as events of the
play's action. They are designed to integrate with the play's verbal images of pain and torture, and thus with the concept that
life is a torture chamber. In terms of the immediate theatrical
effect, we can say that the main experience projected in the
fourth act is that of the torture chamber, a secular crucifixion.
Thence spring its sensations. And its artistic justification lies in
the meaning that may be assigned to the central figure. The
Duchess, I suggest, is the representative of the 'womanish, and
fearefull mankind' to whom Bosola in his last words refers. It is
the nobility of that figure that dominates the horrors to which
she is exposed.

But we cannot leave the matter there. It would not be sufficient to regard sensationalism as a concept that can be satisfactorily restricted to the representation of extreme states of emotion in their 'pure' form. Nor can it refer only to intensely polarized forces, though there is of course much of this too in Webster. (Emotionally, no contrast is more extreme than the deranged outbursts of Ferdinand with the glacial control of the Cardinal in Act ii, Scene v. Morally, no values are more powerfully opposed than the life-values of Antonio and the Duchess—imaged with palms, music, children—and the death-values of the brothers, imaged with poison, corruption, discord, and sterility.)[28] Sensationalism is a part, the most obvious part, of the general process of presenting a dramatic action so as to engage and involve the audience. This process includes the whole range of dramatic techniques, and thus becomes inappropriate for study here. But in a narrower sense, there are techniques that include and border upon sensationalism. There is an indeterminate frontier that separates thorough-going sensationalism from the common run of the dramatist's stock-in-trade, and with Webster certain methods that extend his sensationalism call for consideration. I shall now review some of these methods which permit him to grip and manipulate the emotions of his audience.

1

Of these, perhaps the most important is the mixed mode. By this, I do not refer simply to the presence of comic matter in tragedy, or to serious matter in comedy. I mean the extent to which the values of one mode are allowed to penetrate the values of the other; so that the spectator receives a complex, 'impure' impression. Now the baroque speciality in the mixed-mode form is the tragi-comedy, essentially a compound of pain and pleasure; and on this account Beaumont and Fletcher can still step forward as the most typical dramatists of their era, as they appeared at the time. Their mode is the dramatic equivalent and anticipation of Bernini's *St. Theresa*, the great embodiment of the baroque achievement in expressing visually the fusion of pain and pleasure. The *St. Theresa*, moreover, reminds us of the

28 Irving Ribner, 'Webster's Italian Tragedies', *Tulane Drama Review*, v (1961), 106–15.

baroque taste for the mixture of materials and techniques. Natural daylight, gilt wood rays of 'light', stucco clouds, marble, all come together in the Cornaro chapel. The independence of separate forms, and materials, is lost in baroque art. This mingling of techniques is in turn analogous to the dramatist's mingling of allegory and naturalism. The transitions from one mode to another I shall consider in the following sections.

As for the pain-pleasure sensation, this is a compound quite alien to Webster's mind, and his tragi-comedy is as unlike Fletcher's as it well could be. Webster's version of the mixed mode is the ironic vision: that is, the faculty of presenting events to us that are constantly being revalued by later events, the later events holding the double status of immediate and comparative events. Nothing in Webster stands on its own. The general sense in which this is true of the flow of events in any play is inadequate to describe Webster. Always one looks for the past, or future, link; the image, the character, the event. The images run the play through and through, providing the substance of the dialogue on which all the characters draw; the characters contrast with each other, or their earlier selves; the events uniformly present a pattern of contrast and reversal. A typical example in *The Duchess of Malfi* is Bosola whispering the truth (that Antonio and the children are alive) to comfort and revive the dying Duchess: the event describes a chiasmus with his later bringing of the truth to the dying Antonio—that his wife and children are dead—to make him die the quicker. The prevailing tone ranges from the mocking, to the sour, to the elegiac. The matter is studied in the section on Irony, Parody, and Caricature; I mention it here as an instance of the way in which Webster withholds from us a simple moral apprehension of the action at any time.

2

A closely related quality is transposition—sudden shifts in mood, style, vocabulary. In the interests, if not the name, of variety, the Elizabethan dramatists had developed the technique of never allowing the spectator to settle into a behavioural routine. Webster is especially fond of sharp modulations of language— though, indeed, his flexible lines do not allow any species of mechanical response. The frontier between prose and verse is rapidly crossed and recrossed. Here, for example, is Flamineo's final speech:

> *Flamineo.* I recover like a spent taper, for a flash
> And instantly go out.
> Let all that belong to Great men remember th'ould
> wives tradition, to be like the Lyons ith Tower on
> Candlemas day, to mourne if the Sunne shine, for fear
> of the pittiful remainder of winter to come.
> 'Tis well yet there's some goodnesse in my death,
> My life was a black charnell: I have caught
> An everlasting could. I have lost my voice
> Most irrecoverably: Farewell glorious villaines,
> "This busie trade of life appeares most vaine,
> "Since rest breeds rest, where all seeke paine by paine.
> Let no harsh flattering Bels resound my knell,
> Strike thunder, and strike lowde to my farewell.
> (v. vi. 263–76)

It opens with a line and a half of poetry, the accent of the half-line exquisitely catching its sense. The rambling, half-relevant reference to the Candlemas Day tradition needs and gets prose, whose sprawl communicates the dying man's loss of control. Then Flamineo pulls himself together for a final surge of blank verse, broadening out from an actor's jest to the formality of the *sententia*, 'This busie trade of life. . . .' The clanging rhymes of the final couplet, spoken with a final spasm of energy and control, round off the passage. Webster is here simultaneously exploring the frontiers of the mind and of language.[29]

The several distinct modulations of this passage indicate the disposition of Webster's writing. Always fluid, his dramatic verse never maintains the same pace or accent for long. The fluidity is that of a rapid stream, always moving with a tension and unease, sometimes dropping suddenly and changing level or direction, negotiating with hectic suddenness a mass of rocks, then resuming its troubled flow.

Or consider the classic passage of the Duchess's response to Bosola:

> What would it pleasure me, to have my throate cut
> With diamonds? or to be smothered

---

[29] See also Milton Crane's analysis of the same passage in *Shakespeare's Prose* (University of Chicago Press, Chicago, Ill., 1963), p. 55.

With Cassia? or to be shot to death, with pearles?
I know death hath ten thousand severall doores
For men, to take their *Exits*: and 'tis found
They go on such strange geometricall hinges,
You may open them both wayes: any way, (for heaven sake)
So I were out of your whispering: Tell my brothers,
That I perceive death, (now I am well awake)
Best guift is, they can give, or I can take—
I would faine put off my last womans-fault,
I'ld not be tedious to you.
                                  (IV. ii. 222–33)

The movement of this speech proceeds from the questions—the images are fantastic, but the lines are controlled—to the imposed, stately order of 'I know death hath ten thousand severall doores. . . .' Then the Duchess's nerve and voice break, and she permits herself one uncontrolled cry, the only moment—it lasts a line—when she does not assert a measure of self-control; a pause, and then the careful reimposition of control for the instruction, 'Tell my brothers'—a prince should give orders with firmness and clarity; lastly, the terrible demi-jest of the woman who will not, in death, keep others waiting. The verse's movement is a graph of the mind's.

Other modulations instance the same principle. The staccato brilliance of Ferdinand's 'Cover her face: Mine eyes dazell: she di'd yong' (IV. ii. 281) reveals a disconnected mind, that cannot express itself through conjunctions and adverbs. The line yields to the quiet, elegiac cadence of Bosola's

> I thinke not so: her infelicitie
> Seem'd to have yeeres too many.
>   (IV. ii. 282–3)

The sumptuous rhetoric of Monticelso's 'Shall I expound whore to you?', a cadenza of twenty-three lines, is countered by Vittoria's brazen, deflating 'This carracter scapes me' (III. ii. 82–105). The tone and form of the dialogue never remain unvaried for long.

3

The movement of Webster's language, then, constantly forces the listener to readjust, to experience more intensely, in a word to involve himself in it. But against this must be set a modulation of a quite different order; from the informal to the formal. Webster's taste for the *sententia* is well known. He seems, as Brooke remarks, to have had a particular taste for the intellectual pleasure of generalizing from data.[30] There is more to this, however, than a matter of cast of mind. The *sententiae* exist psychologically as fragments of an older morality, to which Webster's characters refer but cannot adhere. It is evidence of lack of integration. Still, the effect is bound to be a somewhat jarring one for the audience. The characters appear to switch from living *in* the experience to the attempted standing *outside* and drawing conclusions from it. It entails an almost stylistic shift, from informal to formal, and this is a specific theatrical event. It is a distancing effect even if it stops short of what we should nowadays call an alienation effect. Shakespeare employs a somewhat comparable effect, as when he makes Pandarus say:

> If ever you prove false one to another, since I have taken such pains to bring you together, let all pitiful goers-between be called to the world's end after my name; call them all Pandars. Let all constant men be Troiluses, all false women Cressids, and all brokers-between Pandars!
>
> (*Troilus and Cressida*, III. ii. 206–12)

The reference from individuals to types constitutes an odd distancing generalization. The flower distribution and flower talk of *The Winter's Tale* (IV. iv.) impresses upon the spectator that it is part of a very old ritual indeed. Such shifts are, as we should expect, more abrupt and pronounced in Webster. Romelio, in the midst of a general discussion of epitaphs, breaks off the conversation thus:

> Very well then,
> I have a certaine meditation
> If I can think of't, somewhat to this purpose—
> Ile say it to you, while my mother there
> Numbers her Beades.

—and without more ado, launches into his 'meditation'—an extended *sententia* that is Webster's favourite device for commenting on the action (*D.L.* II. iii. 110–47). Similarly, Bosola moves abruptly from a stock satiric tirade against cosmetics (delivered

---

[30] Rupert Brooke, *John Webster and the Elizabethan Drama* (Sidgwick and Jackson, London, 1916), p. 137.

in prose), through 'I do wonder you doe not loath your selves—
observe my meditation now' to the meditation itself,

> What thing is in this outward forme of man
> To be belov'd?
> (II. i. 47–62)

From this grave address, he switches without warning to the
sardonic naturalism of

> Your wife's gone to *Rome*; you two cople, and get you
> To the wels at *Leuca*, to recover your aches.

The theme, be it observed, remains the same throughout—
mortality, disease. The handling of the theme exhibits an extraordinary violence of transposition.

There are several sorts of situation wherein the action pauses,
as it were, for formal comment. One can identify the one-line
sententia; the rhymed couplet; the meditation, primarily a lay
sermon; the apologue (*D.M.*, III. ii. 142–59); and the elegy
(*W.D.*, v. iv. 89–98; *D.M.*, IV. ii. 180–97; *D.L.*, v. iv. 131–46),
which implicitly (and, in *The Devil's Law-case*, explicitly) calls for
a musical accompaniment. To this should be added the masque-
like refrain of Jolenta's in the final scene of *The Devil's Law-case*:

> The Downe upon the Ravens feather
> Is as gentle and as sleeke,
> As the Mole on *Venus* cheeke.
> Hence vaine shew!—I onely care,
> To preserve my Soule most faire.
> Never mind the outward skin,
> But the Jewell that's within:
> And though I want the crimson blood,
> Angels boast my Sister-hood.
> Which of us now judge you whiter,
> Her whose credit proves the lighter,
> Or this blacke, and Ebon hew,
> That unstain'd, keeps fresh and true?
> For I proclaim't without controle,
> There's no true beauty, but ith Soule.
> (v. v. 42–56)

Together, these devices constitute a mass of generalized comment, more or less formal in style, upon the play's action. The
spectator is required to switch constantly from yielding to the

naturalism of the language and presentation, to accepting the stylized and unrealistic comment. It is not the use of any of these devices that makes Webster unique in his time; it is the frequency, variety, and abruptness of the transitions. There is not, I suppose, in the Jacobean drama a more 'involving' scene than that in which the Duchess prattles to her mirror, as Ferdinand creeps up behind her; the emotions of the audience are sucked into the event. There is hardly a more brusque dispersal of naturalism than Bosola's 'observe my meditation now.' The presence of both, in the same play, marks the extent to which Webster is determined to activate the intellect and emotions of the spectator as strongly as possible.

4

This combined assault upon the intellect and emotions takes its most interesting form in the images of the play that are found in *The White Devil* and *The Duchess of Malfi*.[31] The highly complex effect of play references within a play does not lend itself to precise comment, but one has to keep a primary distinction in mind: that between the *idea* of the play and the *effect* upon the audience when that idea is mentioned.

The concept of the world as a stage became extremely popular in the early part of the seventeenth century. Friedrich cites Calderon's *The Great Theatre of the World*, which 'dramatized even in its title one of the key ideas of the baroque: the stagelike vanity of this world'.[32] The world-stage image reaches out towards other ideas. On the one hand, it links with the idea that men are actors, wearers of masks, deceivers and dissimulators. In the political sphere, the sense of the disparity between men's thoughts and actions takes great impetus from the writings of Machiavelli, and is subtly developed by Bacon and Gracian. In the drama, the efforts of the Elizabethans to portray the Machiavel provided a vehicle, however crude, for the extension of the thought. (And by the time it reached its terminus in Iago, the Machiavel had become highly polished and intellectualized.) On the other hand, the world-stage image merges easily with the idea that life is a dream, an illusion. It is not necessary to

---

[31] They are also found in *The Devil's Law-Case*, but have no special importance there. I give the references: I. ii. 133; II. iii. 129; III. iii. 7–8; III. iii. 392–3.

[32] Friedrich, op. cit., p. 57.

quote Prospero's final speech, but Calderon's *Life is a Dream* is not so well known, and I quote from Segismund's speech that closes Act II. :

> So that in this world
> Everyone dreams the thing he is, though no one
> Can understand it. I dream that I am here,
> Chained in these fetters. Yet I dreamed just now
> I was in a more flattering, lofty station.
> What is this life? A frenzy, an illusion,
> A shadow, a delirium, a fiction.
> The greatest good's but little, and this life
> Is but a dream, and dreams are only dreams.[33]

The central situation of the play is Segismund's imprisonment, from which he is temporarily released to enact the charade of princedom. It is the most thorough-going exploration of the idea that we have.

All this, however, was perfectly well known; in fact, a platitude. We have to distinguish, if it is possible, the occasions on which the dramatist compels us to become aware that the play *is* a play. When Jacques remarks that 'all the world's a stage' we can assume that no especially significant dramatic experience is entertained by the audience. It is a thought, or pseudo-thought, that can be swallowed whole (or partially) without reference to the fact that it occurs on the stage. It hardly calls into question the nature of the dramatic experience. It is when the dramatist lingers significantly over the play idea that we need to pause. When the murderers of Julius Caesar speculate on the many occasions wherein the assassination will be re-enacted, it is clear that an experience of a special order is being provoked. Even more daringly, for Cleopatra to speak of 'Some squeaking Cleopatra boy my greatness' is to play amazing tricks with the audience's reactions.

The idea used within the context of the theatre, in short, is very different from the idea as an object of intellectual reference. In its most potent form, the play image has a distancing effect that approaches, but does not cross, the threshold of what we should nowadays term the alienation effect. Very broadly, the alienation

[33] I quote from the English version by Roy Campbell, printed in Eric Bentley, *The Classic Theatre*, vol. iii : *Six Spanish Plays* (Doubleday, Garden City, New York, 1959), 456.

effect can be defined as a sudden change in the conventions through which the play's action is being presented, which is to say a shattering of the illusion that the play is a self-contained entity. In its pure form, this consists of direct address to the audience by the actor. (Apart, naturally, from the formal occasions of prologue, epilogue, and chorus.) As this is very considerably a matter of presentation, one cannot be definitive. There are, for example, ample opportunities for a soliloquy to be delivered as a direct address to the audience, thereby breaking the theatrical convention that the audience does not exist. This would be most unlikely in a serious drama, but it seems quite likely that a clown's soliloquies would, as it were, admit the presence of an audience. (Comedians have always enjoyed a special *rapport* with their audience.) That is an extreme dramatic effect that does not concern us here. Somewhat short of that effect is a succession of references and metaphors based on the play idea, that nudges the audience into an awareness that the dramatic illusion *is* an illusion. Anne Righter's study, *Shakespeare and the Idea of the Play*, has demonstrated Shakespeare's consistent interest in the play metaphor: it seems that he uses it more frequently than any contemporary English dramatist. But all of the metaphors remain within the dramatic conventions. 'All of these indirect references to the audience stem from the mediaeval tradition; all of them take form during that period of transition between 1550 and the early work of Kyd and Marlowe when the play was beginning to establish itself as illusion.'[34]

Such indirect references form part of Webster's manipulation of the audience. For him, as for other dramatists, the play image is both intellectual concept and part of the effect he aims at. He is interested in the linguistic—and psychological—ambivalence of the verb 'to act', and I shall discuss later the sense in which Flamineo and Bosola are to be regarded primarily as role-players. He is also interested in the idea of the futility, the dream-like and illusory quality of life—an idea expressed most strongly, perhaps, in Antonio's dying words (v. iv. 71–82) and finding its most appropriately dramatic form in the echo scene. The voice of the dead Duchess, the crumbling stones, the doomed Antonio, all combine to blur the frontiers of life and death. The idea is

[34] Anne Righter, *Shakespeare and the Idea of the Play* (Chatto and Windus, London, 1962), p. 63.

enforced in the play images that cluster towards the end of *The Duchess of Malfi*. The Duchess's

> And Fortune seemes onely to have her eie-sight,
> To behold my Tragedy . . .
>
> (IV. ii. 37–8)

is suggestive; so are the references to Bosola as an actor (IV. ii. 307–9; v. v. 106); but most powerful is the concluding:

> *Malateste.* Thou wretched thing of blood,
> How came *Antonio* by his death?
> *Bosola.* In a mist: I know not how,
> Such a mistake, as I have often seene
> In a play. . . .
>
> (v. v. 116–20)

The phrase echoes down the vaults of our minds. It is among the most fundamental of all possible assaults that a dramatist can make upon the credulity of his audience, for it questions the very reality of the experience which that audience has been undergoing. The context and emphasis of the final reference put it outside the normal run of more-or-less banal references to the play idea. Webster, at the close of *The Duchess of Malfi*, seeks to jar the audience from its involvement in the play as an imitation of life—while remaining legitimately within the framework of the conventions and of Bosola's character and situation. The effect, the philosophical point, and the psychological point come together.

The idea of the world as stage, dream, or illusion is very baroque, and we need not look far for structural parallels in the visual arts. One might cite El Greco's *The Burial of Count Orgaz*: the point of this painting, necessarily missed in many representations, is that it hangs over the actual tomb of the Count in San Thomé. The mind of the spectator must move from the literal presence of the corpse, through the painterly illusion of the burial, to the reality of heaven as indicated in the painter's illusion. Thus there are three different kinds of reality and illusion. The best analogue to the stage idea is, however, the mirror. Structurally they are completely parallel: the stage image questions the reality of the dramatic experience; the mirror image questions the reality of the visual experience. Parmigianino's distorted *Self-Portrait* (1524) is an early and extraordinarily interesting affair that seems to bring into question the whole nature of reality. Still more fascinating is Velasquez's *Maids of Honour* (1656), a totally assured double trick with the mirror that leaves the viewer to realize that he beholds the scene through the eyes of the King and Queen—who are present in the mirror. Such a device, as with the play images, leaves the viewer with a queasy feeling, as of one whose mental gyroscope has been affected. The sudden shift to a different plane of reality is, psychologically, the hardest of all sensations to take. This feeling, however, cannot persist in an environment of total illusionism. Anne Righter draws attention to the false architectural perspectives of Tiepolo, and to the ceilings of baroque Rome.[35] In Gaulli's interior of Il Gesù (*c.* 1678) the spectator cannot distinguish the walls from the beginning of the ceiling; all is lost in illusion. By 1623 Guercino's ceiling to the Villa Ludovisi had already dated the beginning of a decline of a great idea.

Webster, in fact, might have been a little late even in 1614, the date of *The Duchess of Malfi*. The success of this sort of enterprise depends on an audience that can still distinguish the play's 'reality' from 'illusion'. But *The Duchess of Malfi* follows three years after *The Tempest*: and 'The confusion between actors and audience, illusion and reality which *The Tempest* promulgates is alien to the ordinary Elizabethan attitude towards the spectators. It is, however, the fundamental principle of the masque.'[36]

To sum up. Sensationalism is a central principle of all the arts in the early seventeenth century, to such an extent that one cannot readily criticize its employment without incurring the charge of being unhistorical. From Archer on, the leading critics of Webster have not, in my view, covered themselves against this charge. To do so, very careful distinctions have to be made. It is not legitimate to employ 'sensationalism' as a simple, adverse value judgement. It is necessary to argue, (a) that the sensational devices are improper for the genre; or (b) that their mechanical deployment is unrelated to the serious purposes of the play; or (c) that the devices are ineffective in themselves. These propositions have not been properly argued: they have been stated, or implied. (a) cannot seriously be argued; (c), with regard to certain passages of *The Duchess of Malfi*, may be asserted,

[35] Ibid., p. 207.   [36] Ibid., p. 204.

but in the present state of Websterian productions carries no weight; (b) requires a sufficient analysis of the positive concerns of the dramatist. Such an analysis I attempt in Part Two of this work. The ends-means discussion still dominates the issue here, but that argument needs to go against Webster before sensationalism can be condemned.

This section cannot, therefore, be considered in isolation. But it affords some evidence of the variety and ingenuity of Webster's manipulative devices, beyond the commonplaces of extremes of emotion, horror, and grotesquerie. The subtler devices are, as has been shown, far more interesting. These consist, first, of a mode of presentation in which the action denies a simple response, but insists on an ironic consciousness of time, an awareness that nothing will remain unrevalued by time. Next, the movement of his verse—rapid, flexible, abrupt—parallels the movements of his characters' minds, in whom, as Brooke says, 'you see the instincts at work jerking and actuating them, and emotions pouring out irregularly, unconsciously, in floods or spurts and jets, driven outward from within, as you sometimes do in real people.'[37] The frequent transpositions from this verse movement to the deliberately old-fashioned stiffness of the *sententiae*—from the informal to the formal—induce in us a queer distancing effect. This effect is consummated in the play and actor images, marshalled and deployed for maximum effect at the conclusion of the tragedies. Such images convey not only the concept that life is an illusion, a play, but enforce to the threshold of alienation the sense of the unreality of the action.

[37] Brooke, op. cit., p. 123.

III

IRONY, PARODY, AND CARICATURE

I F sensationalism is an assault on the senses and emotions of the audience, irony is the parallel assault on its intellect. The mode is important to all, I think, drama of the first order, and is central to Webster's work. Irony is, in Northrop Frye's phrase, 'a technique of saying as little and meaning as much as possible'.[38] Hence we can think of it as a means of charging words, actions, and situations with the utmost latent energy. This is ensured by so organizing dramatic events that a given 'form' stands in a significant relationship with a complementary or opposed form. That form may be a person, a situation, an event, or a pattern of language. In essence, then, irony consists of a juxtaposition of whole forms.

Dramatic irony has several varieties. The term usually means, in the first instance, that the words of the speaker may be invested with a double meaning by the events of the future (or past); the audience makes the synthesis. As with words, so with actions and situations. *Peripeteia* is two contrasted situations, presented along a time-scale. Webster composes his tragedies out of a myriad such present-future reversals, of which a sufficient illustration is the Duchess's early remark, 'Yet, should they know it, time will easily scatter the tempest' (I. i. 539–40). Another form of dramatic irony, much favoured by Webster, compresses the reversal into the present; this is the opposition of appearance and reality. Thus, the implications of the title, *The White Devil*, are especially aroused whenever Vittoria is on stage; and the figure is frequently varied, as when the unction-bringing Franciscans are revealed as murderers. These two varieties of irony, temporal and appearance-reality oppositions, account for much of Webster's exploitation of the mode. Instances of the first type of dramatic irony need not be accumu-

[38] Northrop Frye, *Anatomy of Criticism* (Princeton University Press, Princeton, N.J., 1967), p. 40.

lated, nor need we consider the ironies of the appearance-reality opposition, since this has been admirably carried out by Hereward T. Price.[39] But the resources of irony extend further than this.

Irony can take the form of parody and caricature. Now these terms have restricted meanings and it is necessary to lodge a caveat before applying them to a play. Parody is a literary satire, in which an author's characteristics are generally mimicked; caricature, a term whose original use is in the visual arts, grossly exaggerates one or two salient features. These terms (with others, such as burlesque) are inadequate to describe the sustained and inventive vein of allusion, mockery, and suggestive parallel that runs through the Jacobean drama of the first rank. Thus:

(i) Language may parody other modes of language, as when Falstaff prostrates his audience by assuming the vein of Cambyses.

(ii) Plot and subject, or at least two separate actions, may comment on each other. This, as in the two-level clowning of *Dr. Faustus*, may fairly clearly reveal a satiric intention of the author. The actions of the clowns manifest an authorial intention that is matched, in the purely linguistic field, by parody. One should note that the existence of parallel situations does not of itself prove satiric intent. *Hamlet* is a case in point; the three father-son relationships imply a basis for serious comparison, with no hint of mockery.

(iii) Characters, rather than action, may echo each other. The distinction between (ii) and (iii) may on occasion be fine, and not worth detailed scrutiny; but the resemblance between Julia and the Duchess of Malfi may be cited. J. R. Brown convincingly remarks that the omission of Julia would hardly affect the action of the play; she exists as a comment on the Duchess.[40]

What is common to each of these varieties is a comparison

---

[39] Hereward T. Price, 'The Function of Imagery in Webster', *Elizabethan Drama: Modern Essays in Criticism*, ed. R. J. Kaufmann (O.U.P., New York, 1961), pp. 225–49.

[40] J. R. Brown (ed.), *The Duchess of Malfi* (Methuen, London, 1964), p. xli.

(or juxtaposition), whether of language, of action, or of character. I contend that each of these comparisons stems from a certain way of looking at the world, one very well comprehended by the leading dramatists of the era. It is a vision that perceives above all the disparate and irreconcilable elements of life. The critical difficulty is that one should use terms that are conventionally limited to one category only of the three listed above—parody for language, construction for parallelism of action, and caricature for person. But my purpose here is to stress the family likeness of these categories, rather than their separate implications. Current usage extends the verb 'to parody' beyond language to include stage action; this has its attractions, but introduces an idea of mockery and ridicule that may be in excess of the dramatist's intentions. It seems safest to rely on the terms 'parallel', 'echo', and 'comment on'. The issue is important for two reasons. It is always desirable to keep one's categories as restricted, and therefore as useful, as possible. It is also necessary to be aware that parody, parallel construction, and caricature are all manifestations of the same vision or cast of mind.

I should like, then, to emphasize the central importance of the ironic mode, rather than the distinctness of its techniques. But an alternative classification of those techniques may be profitable. Suppose that we dissolve the three categories of comparison, and reclassify the phenomena which they describe into two major categories. One is limited to elements within the play, and the other calls upon material outside the play. Internal and external comparison suggest two differing emphases of ironic intent on the dramatist's part. If we apply the distinction to the three original categories, its usefulness becomes apparent:

(i) Parody reveals a dynamic attitude towards tradition. It normally alludes to external material, and assumes a definite stance. The elements in this situation—original, parody, and attitude of parodist—are normally clearly defined. *The Revenger's Tragedy* is a burlesque morality. Iago is the vice, but aware of it. So, therefore, is his audience (at least, the more sophisticated segment of it). 'And what's he then that says I play the villain?' The relationship with tradition is both distanced and synthesized.

(ii) The technique of parallel actions is much more subtle, because we lack a fixed point. If two actions are parallel, which can be regarded as the true major? A case in point is Ronconi's recent successful production of *The Changeling* in Italy, which made the play's framework the asylum, as in Weiss's *Marat/Sade*.[41] Inversion is, however, all very well as a principle of production; it is not an authorial principle, for in expert dramaturgy the playwright will often mask his viewpoint. In that case he presents alternatives. The play can be interpreted as an 'either/or' statement; or the statement comprises 'either' *and* 'or', making of the collision of viewpoints a pluralist universe. I believe this possibility to be relevant to *The Duchess of Malfi*. In any event, one can agree with William Empson's view of the double plot, that it could 'suggest so powerfully without stating anything open to objection'.[42] It is rather like the anti-libel device of news editors, the juxtaposition of apparently unrelated headlines, photographs, and stories.

(iii) The whole point of caricature is that it must be relatable to the original person; it stands not in its own right, but as a modification of a known person or portrait. There are then two types of caricature in the drama. One relates to a person who is well known in contemporary life, some of whose qualities are seized upon for the dramatic representation. Thus, the Black Knight in Middleton's *A Game at Chess* (1624) was instantly recognized as the Spanish Ambassador, Gondomar (so much so that official protests followed). Again, Horace in Dekker's *Satiromastix* (1601) was a celebrated satire upon Jonson. In the other type, figures that are highly simplified are set down alongside psychologically realistic portraits. Beatrice-Joanna and Isabella, Coriolanus and his butterfly-hunting son are instances. And their interaction sets up in the spectator a double or multiple type of vision, that we are justified in terming ironic. These two forms of caricature are to be distin-

---

[41] Reviewed in *The Times*, 6 May 1967.

[42] William Empson, *Some Versions of Pastoral* (Harmondsworth, Penguin, 1966), p. 34.

guished from two contemporary forms of dramatic portraiture which have at first sight a resemblance. The
flat, typical presentation of character in the comedy of
humours, or the late morality work of Marston and
Tourneur is not caricature, because it does not modify
the lineaments of a credible human being. Nor are
Richard III and Iago caricatures, because full-length
psychological portraits have been built up on the foundation of the vice-figure. They exhibit what Bernard
Spivack terms a 'laminated structure'.

The reclassification that I suggested has the effect of distinguishing between overt and implicit comment. Parody is really
a straightforward and explicit affair; parallel actions are usually
subtle and implicit; caricature may be broad or veiled.

The relevance of this discussion to Webster is most pronounced with implicit comment and with caricature. Neither *The
White Devil* nor *The Duchess of Malfi* can be said to contain a
subplot, or minor action. Nor is Webster much interested in
parodies of language. I incline to agree, however, with James R.
Hunt's interesting suggestion that *The White Devil* contains
three parodies of Christian ritual: that of the marriage service
(Brachiano-Isabella, ii. i); the confession (Lodovico-Monti-
celso, iv. iii); and extreme unction (Lodovico and Gasparo with
Brachiano, v. iii.).[43] These three passages reflect Webster's
keen sense of the ironic, together with an intention to stress the
satanism of the characters. They can, of course, be regarded as
appearance-reality devices, as well as parodies.

The possibilities of internal caricature appear to have engaged Webster's mind very considerably in *The Duchess of Malfi*.
The play contains several personages who appear to exist primarily as satiric commentaries on others. Julia, the great lady
accustomed to take the initiative in wooing has already been
mentioned; she bears a grotesque resemblance to the Duchess.
So, however, does the Old Lady. The opening of the scene (ii. i)
in which she first appears is written solely for its allegoric content, of which Bosola's 'meditation' is the most important part;
otherwise the scene could begin at line 63. She is evidently a re-
tired whore, to judge from Bosola's words. His obscene wit to

43 James R. Hunt, 'Inverted Rituals in Webster's *The White Devil*', *Journal of
English and Germanic Philology*, lxi (1962), 41–7.

her has two themes: her painting of her face, emblematic of
mortality (II. i. 22–41); and her sexual activities (II. i. 42–5;
II. ii. 5–25). His jest about the glass-house, and the swelling-up
of the glass (II. ii. 6–10) is clearly a glancing reference to the
pregnant Duchess, and the glass-house image is taken up by the
second madman. His Boschlike comment—'Hell is a meere
glasse-house, where the divells are continually blowing up
women soules, on hollow yrons, and the fire never goes out'
(IV. ii. 81–3)—has a crazy relevance; the idea of incontinence
and sin is one of the possible viewpoints that we need to bring to
the Duchess. We do not, of course, need to take too seriously
the obscene caricature of womanhood that the Old Lady represents. But she *is* there; her presence reaches out and infects all
women, including the Duchess; the hint is dropped that the
Duchess is not without her taint of corruption. Even old Castruchio fills a minor role in this satiric pantomime. He is coupled
with the Old Lady: 'Here are two of you, whose sin of your
youth is the very patrimony of the Physition. . . .', says Bosola
(II. i. 42–3). This obscene pantaloon serves to damn the other
half of humanity, and enable Bosola to proceed to his disgusted
survey of mankind. Webster uses Castruchio also to strike a
slight blow at Ferdinand; for Bosola advises Castruchio, 'when
you come to be a president in criminall causes, if you smile upon
a prisoner, hang him, but if you frowne upon him, and threaten
him, let him be sure to scape the Gallowes' (II. i. 9–12). This
sounds reminiscent of Ferdinand's judicial methods (I. i. 175–
83). In such scenes Webster seems to be making a deliberate
gesture towards the mode of allegory. Just as Act IV seems to
make Time (Bosola) punish Luxury (the Duchess), so here
Castruchio and the Old Lady seem repulsive masks which are
extensions, and degradations, of Pleasure. One thinks of
Bronzino's *Allegory of Luxury*.[44]

The major comparison in *The Duchess of Malfi* is, however, the
mad scene in Act IV. Miss Inga-Stina Ekeblad has argued convincingly that the eight madmen compose an anti-masque.[45] This
was a grotesque episode which, from 1608–9 onwards, custo-

[44] See also Erwin Panofsky's analysis of that work, in *Studies in Iconology*
(Harper and Row, New York, 1962), pp. 86–90.

[45] Inga-Stina Ekeblad, 'The "Impure Art" of John Webster', in *Elizabethan
Drama: Modern Essays in Criticism*, ed. R. J. Kaufmann (O.U.P., New York, 1961),
pp. 250–67.

marily preceded the main dances of a court masque; it presented
in a distorted form the main theme to follow. The structural details of the anti-masque correspond precisely with those of the
madmen's performance. Thus, the play's opening act, which contains a miniature 'marriage masque', looks forward to Act IV,
which contains a masque of death. Such an opposition is essentially
ironic, since neither episode stands in its own right: if Webster
makes a definitive pronouncement on the action hereabouts, it is
that the Duchess was mad.

> Ambition (Madam) is a great mans madnes,
> That is not kept in chaines, and close-pent-roomes,
> But in faire lightsome lodgings, and is girt
> With the wild noyce of pratling visitants,
> Which makes it lunatique, beyond all cure—
>
> (I. i. 483–7)

says Antonio forebodingly. Cariola's choric observation is
'. . . it shewes/A fearefull madnes' (I. i. 577–8). The reversal
comes in IV. ii, when the Duchess acknowledges her madness:

> nothing but noyce, and folly
> Can keepe me in my right wits, whereas reason
> And silence, make me starke mad. . . .
>
> (IV. ii. 6–8)

And:

Duchess.   When I muse thus, I sleepe.
Cariola.   Like a mad-man, with your eyes open?
                                    (IV. ii. 18–19)

As in *King Lear*, madness-sanity and seeing-blindness are major
themes. Generally, then, the mad scene offers a parody and reversal of the early marriage scene.

But the general contains some specific commentaries. It is
worth considering the identities of the first four madmen. We
are given the calling of all eight, but four of them (tailor, broker,
farmer, usher) seem to relate to nothing else in this play. It is,
however, extremely tempting to speculate on Webster's intentions concerning the other four, each of whom seems to have a
speaking part, though the exact assignment of speeches is open
to controversy.[46] The mad astrologian has a ready analogue in

---

[46] The matter is reopened in Frank B. Fieler, 'The Eight Madmen in *The Duchess
of Malfi*', *Studies in English Literature 1500–1900*, vii (1967), 343–50.

Bosola, who shows himself in II. ii., to be expert in the astrologer's mystery—his instant comprehension of the horoscope, 'Why now 'tis most apparant' (line 81) and readiness to exchange the experts' code-word with Antonio, 'Doe you find it radicall?' (line 30), are most suggestive. We know in any case that he is a speculative scholar (III. iii. 50–7). The lecherous priest bears an obvious resemblance to the Cardinal, and 'I will lie with every woman in my parish the tenth night: I will tithe them over, like hay-cockes' (IV. ii. 84–5) is decidedly reminiscent of the pastoral care exercised by the Cardinal over Julia. The mad doctor is not notably worse than the charlatan who believes he can cure Ferdinand (V. ii). Finally, there is the mad lawyer. At first glance, he appears to have no analogue in the main action of the play. Nevertheless, a plausible law-man can be advanced: Ferdinand. His symbolic role in the drama is that of the perverted justicer, and this role takes literal form early on: Antonio says

> He speakes with others Tongues, and heares mens suites,
> With others Eares: will seeme to sleepe o'th bench
> Onely to intrap offenders, in their answeres;
> Doombes men to death, by information,
> Rewards, by heare-say.

And Delio drives in the point:

> Then the Law to him
> Is like a fowle blacke cob-web, to a Spider—
> He makes it his dwelling, and a prison
> To entangle those shall feede him.
>
> (I. i. 175–83)

The importance of the law theme is fully established in the climactic dialogue between Ferdinand and Bosola across the Duchess's corpse (IV. ii. 311–40), all hingeing on 'was I her Judge?' (322).

　　Astrologian, priest, lawyer, and doctor seem to constitute minor caricatures of Bosola, the Cardinal, Ferdinand, and his doctor. It is not necessary to look for exactitude of parallel—caricature, by definition, is neither fair nor precise. Each miniature, however, derives greater significance from being embedded in a scene which as a whole is now generally conceded to be a serious element of the structure of *The Duchess of Malfi*.

And the general satiric point is that the madmen are not greatly inferior to the play's principals, whom they represent. All four of the major actors are defeated, in terms of their symbolic role. Bosola the star gazer dies conceding the world to be a 'deepe pit of darknesse', beyond which he cannot see; the priest approaches his end in the fear of hell-fire; the judge explicitly renounces his right to judge, and goes mad—a 'fatall judgement', as Bosola observes, on *him*; the doctor can diagnose the ill, but not cure it. The *schema*, surely, is too neat to be coincidental.

The growing sense of the possibilities of irony is perhaps the most interesting literary development of the baroque era. Moreover, one can observe a parallel development in the visual arts. The visual caricature is a baroque development, and is a striking parallel to the dramatic caricatures in *The Duchess of Malfi* that we have considered. However, before commenting on visual caricature, one must note the development of a quality that historically preceded it; the grotesque.

The grotesque (*la grottesca*) refers in the first place to a certain ornamental style, which became fashionable in Italy in the early sixteenth century, and spread in the course of the century throughout northern Europe. Kayser describes thus Raphael's grotesques, commissioned for the pillars of the Papal loggias (*c.* 1515):

. . . curled and involuted shoots, from whose foliage animals emerge and cause the difference between animal and vegetable forms to be eliminated, slender vertical lines on the lateral walls, which are made to support either masks or candelabra or temples, thereby negating the law of statics. The novelty consists not in the fact that, in contrast with the abstract ornamental style, Raphael painted objects from the familiar world (for ornamental combinations of stylized flowers, leaves, and animals had long been used by artists like Ghiberti and his followers), but rather in the circumstance that in this world the natural order of things has been subverted.[47]

The last phrase is especially significant. Thus, the 'grotesque' had for the Renaissance two sorts of implication; the playfully fantastic, and the sinister. The Italians had defined the grotesque as *sogni dei pittori*, and the 'dream' idea allows both implications

[47] Wolfgang Kayser, *The Grotesque in Art and Literature* (Indiana University Press, Bloomington, Ind., 1963), pp. 20–1.

to be present. The sixteenth century exhibits both modes of the grotesque. The playfully fantastic is the Mannerist style, the style of Cellini, Bologna, and Palissy. The sinister depths of the imagination find expression in Hieronymus Bosch and Pieter Breughel.

Growing out of the sixteenth-century taste for the grotesque, the caricature established itself as a form. It is not possible to make satisfying distinctions between the forms—they interpenetrate. Caricature relates primarily to human beings (which the grotesque does not, or not necessarily) and the question is: how far from humanity can one depart, while remaining within the province of caricature?

The question is posed in very practical form by the age-old interest in dwarfs and deformed persons. This interest endured well into the Renaissance: for example, Tietze-Conrat tells us that 'even as late as 1566, thirty-four dwarfs, almost all deformed, served at the banquet given by Cardinal Vitelli in Rome. . . .'[48] Occasionally such people were painted. Thus Bronzino painted two nude studies of the dwarf Morgante, the front and rear view (1553). Eugenia Martinez Vallego executed two paintings of the deformed child Carreño de Miranda (c. 1680), one clothed, one nude. As it happens, we know the facts of the originals, and can therefore state that the paintings are entirely naturalistic. But where we do not know the facts the issue may be in some doubt. It is especially important in the case of Leonardo, some of whose drawings are regarded as prototypes of the caricature form. Are the apparent distortions of the drawing accurate reproductions of a distorted reality, or have they been developed as studies in expression? Tietze-Conrat believes the latter to be true.[49] The question, however resolved, provides us at all events with a serviceable transition, for Tietze-Conrat notes (of Popham's *The Drawings of Leonardo da Vinci*): 'Popham finds it difficult to draw a distinction between portrait and caricature in Leonardo's drawings. Popham is

---

[48] E. Tietze-Conrat, *Dwarfs and Jesters in Art* (Phaidon, London, 1957), p. 14. For further instances of dwarfs in the Italian Renaissance courts, see Enid Welsford's *The Fool* (Faber and Faber, London, 1935), pp. 135–6. Dwarfs figured among the court entertainers in England too. Miss Welsford lists certain entries in the Royal Warrant and Wardrobe accounts for Elizabeth's reign: '. . . a lyttle Blackamore . . . Thomasina the Dwarf . . .' Welsford, p. 170.

[49] Tietze-Conrat, op. cit., p. 16.

right: if freaks are Leonardo's models, then it is only a step from likeness to caricature'.[50]

Caricature proper is, we are told by Gombrich, essentially a baroque invention. 'We have no evidence of portrait caricature before about 1600.'[51] It appears that caricatures were put into circulation by the Carracci about that time; Bernini had to explain the word when he went to Paris in 1665. The systematic distortion and exaggeration of human traits is notably illustrated in the work of Jacques Callot (1592–1635). It seems clear that by the beginning of the baroque era artists were learning to canalize a general taste for the grotesque into the specific genre of caricature, that is to say, an intensified and essentially dramatic form of portraiture.

In fine, the grotesque is a licence to the imagination to explore the implications of the 'real' world. Caricature distorts reality, through the destruction of proportion, and aims at making certain exaggerated and pointed statements about the person identified. These were among the preoccupations of the visual artists of the *Cinquecento* onwards.

There is a strong affinity between the grotesque and caricature. We should expect a taste for the one to nourish the other. This—to return now to the drama—is what in fact we find with Webster. His appreciation of the grotesque is highly individual. I know of no other dramatist of his time with so pronounced a taste for the quality. For Webster, the dramatic embodiment of the grotesque is not so much in incident (though this is certainly true of, say, Flamineo's fake suicide) as in imagery. This consistently depicts a world that coexists alarmingly with the world of the action. Una Ellis-Fermor wrote of the

world called up by the images, a world like that in which the events and characters move, but, by its very wealth of imaginative concentration, less actual—a hidden country which, though full of macabre and hideous, sometimes obscene, forms, is yet a land of escape, into which we wander, are absorbed for a moment, immersed in its fantasy, and from which we return, as from a dream, to the hurry and clash of events.[52]

This is a brilliant, if perhaps overstated, description of Webster's imagery. It is permissible to doubt whether his intentions are

50 Ibid., p. 21.
51 E. Gombrich and E. Kris, *Caricature* (Penguin, Harmondsworth, 1940), p. 10.
52 Una Ellis-Fermor, *The Jacobean Drama* (Methuen, London, 1936), p. 189.

quite so escapist. The 'dream world' may be closer to the world of the action than is here suggested. That world of diseased animals, moving through a landscape of storms and witches to their ultimate retribution, may be Webster's vision of the 'real' world. The psychological objective of the grotesque is the subversion of the natural order; and Webster achieves this most tellingly, perhaps, in Vittoria's dream, wherein the symbolism of the subconscious rises up to threaten the order of the world of society.

At all times Webster is ready to license his imagination to perform an arabesque, a flight of fancy so weirdly compelling that for many readers it has remained *the* Websterian quality. Lodovico, asking Flamineo:

> Wilt sel me fourty ounces of her blood,
> To water a mandrake?
> (III. iii. 109–10)

Bosola's

> I would sooner swim to the *Bermoothes* on
> Two Politisians' rotten bladders, tide
> Together with an Intelligencers hart-string
> Then depend on so changeable a Princes favour.
> (III. ii. 307–10)

Flamineo's 'He carries his face in's ruffe, as I have seene a serving-man carry glasses in a cipres hat-band, monstrous steddy for feare of breaking—He lookes like the claw of a blacke-bird, first salted and then broyled in a candle' (III. i. 76–9), are examples of this trait. Much of it is wild in the extreme; but in the third quotation the imagination has been tethered within the province of caricature—that is to say, Flamineo does make a recognizable observation on the appearance and deportment of the Spanish ambassador.

The most consistently grotesque point made by the imagery is the sustained comparison between human beings and animals. A very great quantity of animal imagery occurs in both *The White Devil* and *The Duchess of Malfi*. Moreover, while in *The White Devil* the animal images form a comment on the dramatis personae that is only suggestive (though very powerfully so), Webster explicitly links the world of man and of animal in the

later play. Bosola's meditation, thematically crucial, brings them
together:

> What thing is in this outward forme of man
> To be belov'd? we account it ominous,
> If Nature doe produce a Colt, or Lambe,
> A Fawne, or Goate, in any limbe resembling
> A Man; and flye from't as a prodegy.
> Man stands amaz'd to see his deformity,
> In any other Creature but himselfe.

(II. i. 47–53)

The animal metamorphosis of Ferdinand drives the point home.
Thus, Webster is pursuing a policy well understood in the visual
arts of the sixteenth and seventeenth centuries, breaking down
the natural barriers between vegetable, animal, and man. Bosch
and the Breughels establish this forcefully; their handling of the
grotesque is similar to Webster's, as Baldini has pointed out.[53]
Mention should also be made of the development of *Knorpelsgroteske* from about 1600 on, which constitutes a dynamic extension of the clear scrollwork style. (*Knorpel*=gristle or cartilage.)
I reproduce Johann Heinrich Keller's *Knorpelsgroteske* of *c.* 1680,
in which the fantastically intertwined heads of men and mon-
sters have lost all firm contours. One would have thought this a
ne plus ultra of grotesque distortion, but the work of Scarfe now
checks the statement. Finally, we must again assert the fundamental tonal distinction in this field, between the playfully fantastic and the sinister. There is no question but that Webster
belongs to the second category.

It remains to appraise the particular quality of irony which is
revealed in Webster's mode of caricature and the grotesque.
For Panofsky, caricature is the expression of a sense of humour—
the comprehension of disparate elements in the universe and in
mankind. It is for him the mode of vision of Cervantes and
Shakespeare. Can such an understanding of 'humour' be applied
to Webster? J. R. Mulryne has discerned a certain quality of
humour in Webster. He writes:

An elusive but unmistakable current of humour is made to play about
almost every scene and incident; it sets at a distance the anarchy the
play embodies and yet in some ways intensifies it, for it is utterly

---

[53] Gabriele Baldini, *John Webster e il linguaggio della tragedia* (Rome, 1953),
pp. 159–63.

corrosive of any value that would seem about to stem the tide of anarchy and give us a resting place for our sympathy.[54]

This, of *The White Devil*, is fair comment, with the reservation that 'humour' requires a broad definition here. It is perfectly possible to argue that 'humour' is a mode of vision that comprehends and reconciles the disparate, whereas the ironic mode perceives only the irreconcilable. Clearly, the latter mode is Webster's. However, the ironic mode need not preclude laughter. As I have suggested, much of *The White Devil* could be played expertly as a *comédie noire*. Not so *The Duchess of Malfi*, whose irony is of an altogether sadder variety. Overall, Webster's irony (whether or not it expects the response of laughter) stops only at his ultimate value, 'integrity of life'. That value is not subject to the corrosion of irony.

To sum up, one could readily devote a volume to the analysis of Webster's variations of irony, and I seek here to emphasize his concern with the techniques of parody and caricature. They accompany a taste for the grotesque, a taste strongly emphasized in Webster's recurring animal imagery. In *The White Devil*, certain rituals of religion are parodied. In *The Duchess of Malfi*, a set of implicit comparisons is drawn between the major and minor characters. One can call this caricature; but since the comparisons extend to activities as well as character (the wooing of Julia and the Duchess) I do not press the term. Parallel and juxtaposition are the essence of the process. It bears a resemblance to the contemporary development of caricature in the visual arts, a phenomenon which should be noted if its relationship cannot be explained. Finally, the artistic validity of irony still requires justification, as I implied earlier, if its constant deployment is not merely a set of nihilistic tricks. Irony is in great part an awareness of time; and time is an expression of death. The ironic technique is especially well adapted to a philosophy that disclaims final knowledge, and depicts man as a unit of consciousness in an 'absurd' universe. The proper extension of an ironic view of human actions is a view of the universe that is equally ironic. This view, in his greatest play, Webster supplies.

[54] J. R. Mulryne, '*The White Devil* and *The Duchess of Malfi*', in *The Jaocbean Theatre*, ed. J. R. Brown and B. Harris (Edward Arnold, London, 1960), p. 207.

IV

CHARACTER

THE Woelfflin categories of the baroque are by no means inapplicable to the drama. Nothing could be more appropriate to the theatre of Shakespeare than Woelfflin's observation (of Rembrandt): '. . . it powerfully supports the illusive effect if an independent activity in the building up of the picture is assigned to the spectator.'[55] This attention to the spectator is part of the movement of the times. There is, in about 1600, a turning away from the general Renaissance proposition that beauty is an objective quality of the work of art. Increasingly it became appreciated that the value of the work lies in the effect produced on the beholder—a subjective, impressionistic aesthetics. Painting and drama afford us here a legitimate field of comparison: the depiction of the human mind. Portrait and character-study in the baroque era reveal the artist and dramatist equally willing to assign a major role to the spectator.

For Rembrandt, *chiaroscuro* is far more than a technical device; it enables the infinite possibilities behind the human face to be suggested. Of Rembrandt, especially, is Woelfflin's statement true: 'The Baroque avoids this acme of clarity. It will not say everything where it can leave something to be guessed.'[56] And again: '. . . beauty no longer resides in fully apprehensible clarity at all, but passes to those forms which cannot quite be apprehended and always seem to elude the spectator.'[56] In what sense do we know the mind of, say, *The Man in the Golden Helmet*—or, for that matter, the Rembrandt of any of the self-portraits? The method of presenting humanity in Shakespeare is exactly parallel. The idea that Shakespeare presents a defined 'character' is, of course, totally misleading. He does nothing of the sort. He has left us primarily a set of stage directions, hints for productions. His text does not delineate character, but sug-

[55] Woelfflin, *Principles of Art History*, p. 28.
[56] Ibid., p. 198.

gests depth possibilities. The words are a *Gestalt*, filled severally by the producer, actor, and spectator. The simplest instance will suffice. One's whole reading of the 'character' of Henry V turns on the line: 'May I, with right and conscience, make this war?' There is no means of locating the nebulous 'character' from which this stems. Are the lines spoken with the brisk, eager zest of a young man impatient to have the last obstacles removed before he can have his war? Or do they illuminate the *Realpolitik* of a prince knowing well that policy can use legality and morality? Or do they reveal the agonized hesitation of a ruler almost crushed by the weight of the dread responsibility that is his? All these, and more possibilities are contained in the text; and perhaps in the man; it is not, in our time, possible to refer to 'character' as an entity capable of absolute definition.

If we apply these ideas to Webster we find a similar blurring of outline. Partly this can be traced to an avoidance of a final statement that indubitably sums up a character. Final statements there always are, but they may be unconvincing (is Bosola's faith in his 'owne good Nature' justified?) or enigmatic ('let me/Be layd by, and never thought of'). Certainly we have, especially in *The Duchess of Malfi*, 'carracters' that serve as constructional devices, useful guidelines to the audience; but they are beginnings, not ends. But the blurring of outline is accomplished very considerably through the use of imagery, which sets up a suggestive undertow to the surface of the speaker's words and actions.

Vittoria is an excellent instance of this method. How are we to regard her? Is she everything that Monticelso claims, or is her magnificent performance on the brink of death a true index to her character? Our emotions are deeply engaged; we sway first one way, then the other. This balance is described thus by M. C. Bradbrook: 'There is, as it were, a subordinate side of Vittoria which is innocent. Actually, she is guilty, but there is a strong undercurrent of suggestion in the opposite direction. It never comes to the surface clearly but it is there. Her character is "reconciliation of opposites".'[57]

And yet, on precisely the same evidence, I should arrive at the opposite conclusion. I should say: Vittoria is innocent, but the imagery damns her as guilty. This may at first appear an

[57] Bradbrook, op. cit., p. 187.

extraordinary statement. Vittoria, it may be urged, is 'obviously' guilty. I ask, of what? On the evidence given in the play, no jury would convict her of anything but the attempted murder of Flamineo (and a good defence counsel would get her off, on the plea of self-defence). Vittoria did not kill Camillo or Isabella; Brachiano did, through his agents. She may have incited him, but the text is ambiguous; nothing is proved; the actress can play it either way. She may have had foreknowledge of the murder; Francisco advises Monticelso to drop the charge. She may have committed adultery with Brachiano; Monticelso cannot prove it, circumstantial evidence notwithstanding. She marries Brachiano afterwards; that is neither a sin nor a crime.

Against each of the charges brought against Vittoria, we must on the evidence of the text bring in a verdict of 'not proven'. But the imagery damns her. The title apart, she is a disease; a wolf; a hawk; a devil under a fair skin. Examples are manifold. The conclusion is clear: Webster knows that she is guilty, and constantly fixes her guilt in the imagery. As a man of the theatre, he keeps her guilt as an undercurrent, and does everything possible on the surface to secure for her our sympathies. Precisely the same method is employed towards the other malefactors. Our sympathies may be engaged, but the imagery constantly asserts their evil.

The full mastery of the Websterian character-presentation is revealed in *The Duchess of Malfi*. He builds up a character-*Gestalt* carefully. First comes a charcoal sketch, the Act 1 'carracter', then the overlaying of the personage's words and actions, together with the colouring of imagery and the slighter (but no less important) 'carracter' observations of other personages. Thus, in Act 1 we have Antonio's 'ethereal' miniature of the Duchess, stressing her continence and holiness:

> But for their sister, (the right noble Duchesse)
> You never fix'd your eye on three faire Meddalls,
> Cast in one figure, of so different temper
> For her discourse, it is so full of Rapture,
> You onely will begin, then to be sorry
> When she doth end her speech: and wish (in wonder)
> She held it lesse vaine-glory, to talke much,
> Then your pennance, to heare her: whilst she speakes,
> She throwes upon a man so sweet a looke,

That it were able raise one to a Galliard
That lay in a dead palsey; and to doate
On that sweete countenance: but in that looke,
There speaketh so divine a continence,
As cuts off all lascivious, and vaine hope.
Her dayes are practis'd in such noble vertue,
That sure her nights (nay more her very Sleepes)
Are more in Heaven, then other Ladies Shrifts.
Let all sweet Ladies breake their flattring Glasses,
And dresse themselves in her.
                                    (I. i. 191–209)

Over this is superimposed the perfectly obvious evidence of her
sensuality: explicit in her relations with Antonio, and 'filtered'
by Ferdinand: 'Growne a notorious Strumpet' (II. v. 6), 'con-
veyances for lust' (II. v. 14), 'If thou doe wish thy Leacher may
grow old/In thy embracements' (III. ii. 117–18), etc.: and
Bosola:

        and this restraint
    (Like English Mastiffes, that grow feirce with tying)
    Makes her too passionately apprehend
    Those pleasures she's kept from.
                                    (IV. i. 14–17)

The 'divine' Duchess takes a brusque line with the Church when
it suits her. Of her private wedding ceremony she asks:

    What can the Church force more?
    . . . How can the Church build faster?
                                    (I. i. 558, 562)[58]

And her decision to make a 'feigned pilgrimage' to Ancona
meets with Cariola's disapproval and a violent reaction: 'Thou
art a superstitious foole' (III. ii. 367). Again, while the 'carracter' stresses her femininity, the Duchess uses several images of
war that suggest the masculine and dauntless side of her nature.
For instance,

            And even now,
    Even in this hate (as men in some great battailes

[58] Concerning the 'guilt' of the Duchess in remarrying, the matter has been
debated by F. W. Wadsworth, 'Webster's Duchess of Malfi in the light of some
Contemporary Ideas on Marriage and Re-marriage', *Philological Quarterly*, xxxv
(1956), 394–407, and by Clifford Leech, 'An Addendum on Webster's Duchess',
Philological Quarterly, xxxvii (1958), 253–6. The point, surely, is that it can be
debated. The issue is debatable, and is meant to be so experienced by the audience.

By apprehending danger, have atchiev'd
Almost impossible actions: I have heard Souldiers say so),
So I, through frights, and threatnings, will assay
This dangerous venture:

(I. i. 384–9)

Also III. ii. 186–8; III. v. 121–2; III. v. 167; and IV. i. 106. Small
wonder that Bosola, in the elegiac survey of her life that precedes her execution, can say:

> A long war disturb'd your minde,
> Here your perfect peace is sign'd.

(IV. ii. 186–7)

Nothing stated in Antonio's 'carracter' of the Duchess is necessarily untrue, yet everything in it has been sharply modified.
The interplay of light and shade can imply a statement, or its
reverse.

It is, moreover, true of the Duchess as of the other personages
that 'The very existence of the baroque figure . . . is bound to
the other motives in the picture. Even the single portrait head is
inextricably woven into the movement of the background, be it
only the movement of light and dark.'[59] The image motifs affect
all the characters, with differences of emphasis. Thus, Ferdinand's animal images merely intensify the theme of human animality, which (as Bosola asserts in his meditation, Act II, Scene
i) includes the whole of humanity: Cariola's comment on the
'madness' of the Duchess extends to the mad-deaf-blind images
that run throughout the play: the images of contract, payment,
reward, and punishment that run through *The White Devil* affect
all the major characters. No Websterian figure is isolable.

This blurring of outline can be traced to other factors. There
is, in Webster, a wild oscillation between extremes of behaviour
within the same person. Flamineo, who likes to think of himself as a materialist bent only upon self-advancement, twice
abandons his course for a wayward impulse of generosity and
honour. He is ready to fight Lodovico for calling his sister a
whore (III. iii. 105–20): he inexplicably defies his lord, Brachiano, when that same fatal word is again flung at him (IV. ii.
45–58). It is, to put it mildly, inconsistent to act as pander to
one's sister, and then be ready to fight with anyone who will

[59] Woelfflin, *Principles of Art History*, p. 169.

apply the appropriate term to that sister; but it is the inconsistency of life, not that of careless dramaturgy. Again, when Brachiano is dead, and can do no more to advance Flamineo, the latter comes out with a quite astounding observation:

> I cannot conjure; but if praiers or oathes
> Will get to th'speech of him: though forty devils
> Waight on him in his livery of flames,
> I'le speake to him, and shake him by the hand,
> Though I bee blasted.
>
> (v. iii. 211–15)

He surprises us; he surprises himself. Of this sort of behavioural spasm, Brooke well observes that 'you see the instincts at work jerking and actuating them, and emotions pouring out irregularly, unconsciously, in floods or spurts and jets, driven outward from within, as you sometimes do in real people.'[60]

Behaviour leads us to the heart of the enigma, identity itself. The problem of identity becomes, with Webster, acute. His characters probe themselves for identity. 'Who am I?' asks the Duchess (iv. ii. 122). 'I have a strange thing in mee, to th'which/ I cannot give a name, without it bee/Compassion' wonders Flamineo. And the account they give of themselves is unsatisfactory. We cannot believe that Ferdinand's policy is to gain 'An infinite masse of Treasure' from the Duchess's death (iv. ii.304); we believe that he has grossly deceived himself. A suspicion remains at the end of *The Duchess of Malfi* that Bosola's faith in his 'owne good Nature' may be misplaced. The same may be said of Shakespeare: does Othello satisfy us at the last when he asserts that he is 'not easily jealous'? He *thinks* he is not. But with Webster the gap between statement and acceptance opens wider.

The actor who portrays a major Websterian character must reconcile the prevailing imagery with baffling inconsistencies of behaviour, and highly dubious 'final' statements of character. This, I believe, is technically perfectly analogous to the use of *chiaroscuro* by a baroque portraitist. But behind the technique is an attitude. The portraitists of the *Cinquecento* see what they see, and know what they know. There is surely no doubt in Holbein's mind that he *knows* Henry VIII: and his art depicts to the limit of his technique that certainty. The polished surfaces of Bron-

---

[60] Brooke, op. cit., p. 123.

zino's society portraits indicate, with reservations, that the qualities of the surface are a fair index to the sitter. Van Dyck does not know the Abbé Scaglia, or Rembrandt, himself—and their art admits as much. This uncertainty is mirrored in the growing popularity of the triptych-portrait, developed though not invented in the baroque era. Commissioned frequently as aids to sculptors, they expressed a concept familiar to the baroque sculptors, most especially Bernini, that there is no absolute standpoint from which to view a three-dimensional portrait. De Champaigne's triptych of Richelieu is a simple quantitative statement of the idea that one man has many faces, and that not one is final.[61] That idea is one that Webster, pre-eminently, shared with his era.

[61] Compare also Lotto's portrait of a man in three positions (now at the Kunsthistorisches Museum, Vienna); Van Dyck's triptych of Charles I (the Queen's Gallery, Buckingham Palace); and Kneller's study of the 2nd Earl of Nottingham (the National Portrait Gallery).

V

MULTIPLICITY AND UNITY

ONE of Woelfflin's five categories of baroque art relates to multiplicity and unity. He asserts that classic (i.e. Renaissance till mid-sixteenth century) art is distinguished by careful articulation of parts. Each part of a work of art from this period is capable of separate analysis. Baroque, on the contrary, projects the total art-work in such a way that analysis of parts no longer seems adequate.

A head by Rubens is not better, seen as a whole, than a head by Dürer or Massys, but that independent working-out of the separate parts is abolished which, in the latter case, makes the total form appear as a (relative) multiplicity. The Seicentists envisage a definite main motive, to which they subordinate everything.[62]

The application of this principle to the early seicentist drama concerns the play's verbal imagery, and its connection with the visual imagery of the action. This is the multiplicity within unity of the drama. It is now a critical commonplace that the pattern of a play's verbal images, linked with its action, is a form of dramatic construction in itself. Over the past thirty years, the tendency of criticism has been to perceive the unifying construction adopted by the major Jacobean dramatists. One does not, nowadays, stress the idea of the Jacobean play as a succession of 'big' scenes, tenuously connected by more-or-less competent dramatic craftsmanship. The best way in to an appreciation of a play's unity is normally through a study of its verbal imagery. Since the seminal work of Caroline Spurgeon, Wilson Knight, and Wolfgang Clemen appeared in the 1930s, many studies on the imagery of the early seventeenth-century dramatists have appeared. Nevertheless, the field has been by no means exhaustively tilled. Webster's imagery, in particular, still lacks a full-length analysis.[63]

[62] Woelfflin, *Principles of Art History*, p. 156.
[63] Partial studies have appeared in Elizabeth Holmes, *Aspects of Elizabethan*

The reason for this is evident if one begins to undertake an analysis. It lies in the density and complexity of Webster's imagery. On my count,[64] there are over 500 images in each of Webster's major tragedies; and some 270 in *The Devil's Law-Case*. This is to be compared with Shakespeare, for whom 339, we are told, stands as the highest number of images in a single play (*Troilus and Cressida*).[65] I shall defer to a later chapter a consideration of what I conceive to be the main themes of these images; here I wish to emphasize the extraordinary density of texture. One is accustomed to think of Shakespeare's plays as being exceptionally rich in imagery; to encounter a dramatist with a 50 per cent greater density calls for comment. Webster seems almost to *think* in images, or to codify his thoughts in images. It is possible to point to long passages in his tragedies

---

Imagery (Blackwell, Oxford, 1929;) M. C. Bradbrook, *Themes and Conventions of Elizabethan Tragedy* (C.U.P., Cambridge, 1935); Una Ellis-Fermor, *The Jacobean Drama* (Methuen, London, 1936); Moody M. Prior, *The Language of Tragedy* (Columbia University Press, New York, 1947); and in the introductions to John Russell Brown's editions of *The White Devil* (Methuen, London, 1960) and *The Duchess of Malfi* (Methuen, London, 1964).

[64] Any system of image-counting is necessarily an impressionistic and imprecise affair. The statistics that I offer should be regarded not as quasi-scientific statements, but as guides to interpretation. Their function is to indicate a trend, and to initiate a train of thought. I have adopted the principles and methods of image-counting outlined by Caroline Spurgeon in Appendix I of *Shakespeare's Imagery* (C.U.P., Cambridge, 1935), with two provisos:

(a) My canon has been conservative throughout. The definition of an image: 'a figure of speech, especially simile or metaphor' is hard to sustain in Webster's writings. His language constantly slides over the frontier between literal and metaphorical statement. I should suggest, as a guiding definition of imagery, 'language whose purpose is other than a literal statement of fact: whose aim is to evoke associations over and above the needs of narrative action'. Dead metaphors and (in Empson's phrase) 'subdued' metaphors pose their usual problems, those dealing with daily life and domestic affairs being especially troublesome. These I have preferred to exclude.

(b) A favourite trick of Webster's is to construct a dialogue in which one character takes up an image from the lips of another. Thus:

Antonio. There is a sawcy, and ambitious divell
            Is dauncing in this circle.
Duchess. Remove him.
Antonio. How?
Duchess. There needs small conjuration, when your finger
            May doe it:

(*The Duchess of Malfi*, I. i. 471–6)

Such cases I count as a single image.

[65] Appendix II, 'The Total Number of Images in each of Shakespeare's Plays', from Spurgeon, op. cit., p. 361.

that are virtually devoid of ordinary, indicative statements. The difficulties placed in the way of the reader are acute, for very great demands on his powers of assimilation are made. Yet without assimilating the drifts of the imagery, no adequate response to Webster can be made.

The spectator, however, has a resource not fully open to the reader. He can see and apprehend the details of the action; and the implications of the visual symbolism reverberate with the implications of the verbal. The total effect of a Webster production, as is perfectly clear from the texts that Webster has left us, is designed to be very different from the effect derived solely from reading the play.

This is an old critical battlefield, and it is worth noting that in practice Webster has come off badly. No judgement on Webster's powers as a master of the theatre is proper until the day when Webster is accorded a place in the permanent repertory of the great professional companies. Any comparison with Shakespeare (for example, the relative effectiveness of the last scenes in *Hamlet* and *The Duchess of Malfi*) is totally misleading. Shakespeare gets, quite simply, the best productions. He is cut judiciously—hardly anyone has ever seen an uncut Shakespeare production. Producers devote a large proportion of their careers to studying the rhythms, the emphases, the reticences, the meanings, the ambiguities of a Shakespeare play. Actresses have to learn how to overcome such cruces as delivering 'Kill Claudio' without raising a laugh. Such standards are not as yet possible for Webster. On the celebrated 'theatrical effectiveness' of Webster I have, therefore, nothing to say, since the matter has never been decisively demonstrated. The critics who applaud his *coups-de-théâtre*, and those who emphasize only to decry his theatrical skill, proceed equally upon faith. Without a sequence, not too far separated in years, of performances by the best actors and leading producers, adequately canvassed by the metropolitan critics, no convincing judgement is possible. Isolated performances by university amateur dramatic companies are suggestive but clearly demonstrate little. My concern here is merely to point out that Webster's texts are above all designed for performance. We have, after all, his own view on the matter: 'A great part of the Grace of this (I confesse) lay in Action; yet can no Action ever be gracious, where the decency of the Language, and Ingenious structure of the Scaene, arrive not to make up a perfect Harmony.'[66]

The terminology for examining the 'ingenious structure' of the scene, together with the 'decency of the language', comes readily to hand. Hereward T. Price has analysed Webster's imagery in terms of a double structure, 'figure-in-word' and 'figure-in-action'. He found an 'exact and sustained correlation' between the 'outer and inner figure' in Webster; that is, a 'double construction'. After examining *The White Devil* and *The Duchess of Malfi* in the light of this approach, he concluded:

> Figure-in-action and figure-in-word reinforce one another. He repeats himself tirelessly, spinning innumerable variations with his figures of the magnificent outer show and the inner corruption, of life, fortune, hopes that look so fair and delude us utterly, of the many bitter, twisted ironies of the difference between appearance and reality.[67]

With the device in his hands, Mr. Price could have gone much further than this. Webster does indeed use consistently the double construction, but this method is very far from being confined to the single theme that Mr. Price rightly names. This can be demonstrated if we apply the device to the two major tragedies—*The Devil's Law-Case* adopts a different variant of the same method, and requires separate consideration.

THE WHITE DEVIL

Two major themes of *The White Devil* are those of corruption (together with poison, physic, and death) and the Law. 'Not to be weary with you', as Lucio says—for I shall consider these themes more carefully in Part Two—I shall content myself here with pointing out the figures-in-action. Poison, the emblem of the moral evil rife in the play, accounts for Isabella and Brachiano. Nor is this a mere *frisson*: the poisoning of Brachiano embodies

---

[66] Webster's 'To the Juditious Reader' of *The Devil's Law-Case*. Lucas, ii. 236.

The recent history of Websterian stage-production can be studied in Don D. Moore's chapter on 'Webster and the Modern Stage' in his *John Webster and his Critics 1617–1964* (Louisiana State University Press, Baton Rouge, La., 1966), pp. 151–60. It does not make reassuring reading. But the recent successful production of *The White Devil* (1969), in which the full resources of the National Theatre were deployed with the utmost panache, offers a promising late report. It suggests that Webster, given proper handling, can survive very well on the contemporary stage.

[67] Price, op. cit., p. 248.

the theme of retribution, and the extension of the scene into the malignant unction of Ludovico and Gasparo permits the appearance-reality motif again to be presented. The images of retribution find their major embodiment in the great central dramatic image of the play—the trial. Fittingly, the trial ensures a rough but perverted justice. The judicial procedures of Monticelso and Francisco are a travesty of true justice, but the answer they arrive at—banishment to a House of Convertites—is sufficiently appropriate. Revenge, the wild justice that terminates the play, is a form of action parallel to the trial. What is worth stressing here is that the trial is not merely a theatrical showpiece, an equivalent of the Papal election. It presents to us one of the major concerns of the play's action.

Other, less central, instances of the double construction remain. Mention has already been made of the three inverted rituals of confession, marriage, and extreme unction, that integrate with the play's many references to 'devils'. And the images relating to the incompetence of physicians find their expression in the failure of Brachiano's doctor to save him.

THE DUCHESS OF MALFI

The double construction is developed to a very high degree in this play. The extraordinary number of parallelisms and interconnections between plot and imagery is, so far as I know, entirely without precedent or successor in our dramatic annals. The structure is altogether more complex than that of *The White Devil*, and I give here the main categories of figure-in-word and figure-in-action, not necessarily in order of importance:

1. *Appearance-reality*. Since the whole action is a sustained series of reversed hopes and appearances, there is little point in giving detail here. The images of appearance-reality are discussed in Part Two.

2. *Animalism*. The play teems with images of animals, which collectively make a sustained comment on the nature of man, most especially Ferdinand. His lycanthropy activates the images in the most direct way. As Travis Bogard well observes, 'when Ferdinand goes mad, the image becomes actuality . . . Ferdinand *is* an animal.[68]

[68] Travis Bogard, *The Tragic Satire of John Webster* (University of California Press, Berkeley, Calif., 1955), p. 137.

3. *Poison and Corruption.* The many images of poison, corruption, and sickness stem from the play's opening lines:

> *Antonio.*   A Princes Court
> Is like a common Fountaine, whence should flow
> Pure silver-droppes in generall: But if't chance
> Some curs'd example poyson't neere the head,
> "Death, and diseases through the whole land spread.
>
>   (I. i. 12–16)

The 'curs'd example . . . neere the head' consists of Ferdinand and his brother. Via the Cardinal, the corruption motif finds a physical outlet in the poisoning of Julia. Ferdinand's mental sickness destroys both him and the other major personae.

4. *Physic and Physicians.* The related images of physic and physicians (see Part Two, pp. 117–19) all assert the futility of medicine to counter corruption. This is shown in the failure of the doctor who treats Ferdinand. Significantly, the doctor correctly diagnoses Ferdinand's malady, but is powerless to cure.

5. *The Storm.* A score of images of tempest, earthquake, and thunder occur. It is clear that they contribute to the idea of unnatural violence that pervades the play. More importantly they stand for retribution. These images touch on all the characters, but especially Ferdinand.

> . . . time will easily
> Scatter the tempest.
>
>   (I. i. 539–40)

says the Duchess of her brothers' reaction to her marriage. Ferdinand's reaction is to embody in himself Nature's violence.

> Why doe you make your selfe,
> So wild a Tempest?

asks the Cardinal.

> *Ferdinand.*   Would I could be one,
> That I might tosse her pallace 'bout her eares,
> Roote up her goodly forrests, blast her meades,
> And lay her generall territory as wast,
> As she hath done her honors.
>
>   (II. v. 23–9)

The images find their apotheosis in Ferdinand's death. We are told:

> Grisolan. 'Twas a foule storme to-night.
> Roderigo. The Lord *Ferdinand's* chamber shooke like an Ozier.
> Malateste. 'Twas nothing but pure kindnesse in the Divell,
> To rocke his owne child.
> (v. iv. 23–6)

Thus death is for him, as for the others, literally a 'storme of terror'.

6. *The Body.* (a) In Bosola's crucial speech to the Duchess in iv. ii. 123–31, the body is thrice likened to a prison. (Other images of 'prison' occur in the play, notably the ominous one of i. i. 361.) The Duchess is herself in prison, soon to escape from it as from her body.

(b) The comparison between the body and a ruined building is first suggested by Cariola. The Duchess is

> some reverend monument
> Whose ruines are ever pittied.
> (iv. ii. 35–6)

This image is later expanded into a figure-in-action, the echo scene of v. iii.[69] The purpose of this scene is to dramatize the parallel between the body and a ruined building.

> Churches, and Citties (which have diseases like to men)
> Must have like death that we have.
> (v. iii. 19–20)

muses Antonio, drawing the parallel for us. The idea is rounded off later by Bosola's dying words:

> We are onely like dead wals, or vaulted graves,
> That ruin'd, yeildes no eccho:
> (v. v. 121–2)

The image is two-sided. If the body is a ruin, the soul is an echo. The peculiar merit of the echo scene is that Webster has succeeded in dramatizing both halves of the metaphor. It is a notable example of Webster's technique of establishing the most

---

[69] The echo scene is a very baroque device. Its counterpart is in music. There, use is frequently made (as in Monteverdi) of echo effects suggesting the vastness of a church interior, and playing (in choral contexts) on words.

intimate of relationships between plot and image. Moreover, the scene remains a legitimate phase in the broad movement of the play. It is a beautifully timed moment of calm and reflection, reminding one oddly of the quiet discourse between Hamlet and Horatio before he goes on to fight Laertes—and of the philosophizing of the grave-digger scene.

7. *Learning*. Man's quest for knowledge is a theme running through *The Duchess of Malfi*. To this theme, the images of science and philosophy, especially astrology, are related. This theme depends on the interaction of plot, character (Bosola, doctor, first madman) and image: the details of this contention I argue in Part Two, pages 132–6. The main figure-in-action is the horoscope scene—an unsuccessful attempt at reading the stars, for the baby whose future is so darkly forecast actually survives the play; he is the 'young hopefull Gentleman' who turns up with Delio. The other main figure for the baffled quest for knowledge is the Cardinal's laying aside of his theological book, as he enters the last scene.

8. *Darkness*. The 'deepe pit of darknesse' in which mankind dwells is suggested by many images of shadows, eclipses, winter, and death. They blend well with the stage background, which for the most part is explicitly night. The Duchess and Antonio woo at nightfall; the horoscope scene is at night; the discovery of the Duchess's secret takes place at night; so does the whole of the fourth act; and the final scenes are played out against a backdrop of darkness that actually contributes to the action. The literal and symbolic fuse completely.

I contend that these repeated instances of double construction present a formidable proof of Webster's technical competence in this, his most mature artistic product. One or two examples, viewed separately, might appear as happy and casual harmonizations of plot and image. But the number of such instances does not admit of coincidence. The technical difficulties which such a method presents to the playwright are manifestly great; and the result appears to me a technical triumph, even if one ignores all considerations of poetry and psychology—qualities which are sometimes held to be Webster's sole saving graces.

Webster, more than any of his contemporaries, exemplifies the baroque principle of multiplicity and unity; he also, and

necessarily, poses the most arduous problems of analysis. That is
because the texture of his imagery, allied to his plot construction,
is so thick. A study must be analytic, for the synthesis is the play;
yet analysis is doomed to inadequacy. Wolfgang Clemen, writing of Shakespeare, has issued a warning that is relevant here:
'An isolated image, an image viewed outside of its context is only
half the image. . . . It appears as a cell in the organism of the
play, linked with it in many ways'.[70] Virtually any quotation from
Webster will contain an image, which cannot be dealt with in
isolation; and this is a danger constantly run by critics who quote
without identifying the cellular context. To take only two
examples, Ferdinand's 'Cover her face: Mine eyes dazell: she di'd
yong' (IV. ii. 281) has frequently been cited as the sort of thing
Webster is best at, an isolated *coup-de-théâtre*. But it is not: the
eye image looks back to Ferdinand's 'Yes, if I could change/
Eyes with a Basilisque' (III. ii. 101–2) and forward to 'I have
cruell sore eyes' (v. ii. 62). Again, R. W. Dent unluckily singles
out the description of Ferdinand's judicial methods (I. i. 175–
83) for this question:

Yet, actually, it has little strict relevance to the subsequent development of the play. It describes a species of unjust prince or magistrate,
irresponsible and selfish in his distribution of rewards and punishments, an abuser of law very familiar to readers of Webster. But how
much has this to do with the tragedy?[71]

To this one can answer that Webster is deeply concerned, in all
three plays that we know to be solely his, with the Law both as
a literal process and a symbol; and that in *The Duchess of Malfi*,
the dialogue between Ferdinand and Bosola on the nature of
justice and responsibility is the intellectual climax of the play
(IV. ii. 311–42). It also provides two of the sharpest ironies in
the play, with Bosola giving up his moral autonomy to the justicer—who explicitly renounces his right to judge.

The point of the great bulk of Webster's images is that they oper-
ate multilaterally, calling on several groups of images simultaneously. They can look backwards or forwards in time, often with

[70] Wolfgang Clemen, *The Development of Shakespeare's Imagery* (Methuen,
London, 1951), p. 4.
    [71] R. W. Dent, *John Webster's Borrowing* (University of California Press,
Berkeley, Calif., 1960), p. 27.

an ironic implication. The effect is one of diversity, complexity, and yet, unity.

And again, if one considers those images that convey above all tone, one finds, especially in *The Duchess of Malfi*, practically no imagery that seems distracting, at odds with the larger purposes of the author. The use of the commonplace book is not a loose indulgence, but a rigid, almost formal, exercise. To give some examples: I find (in *The Duchess of Malfi*) many images of pain and sickness, but none suggesting the sensations of pleasure. The body is seen as rotten and mortal, not as beautiful and vital. Knowledge is invariably associated with doubt or bafflement, never certainty. With a few exceptions only, those of certain kinds of birds, the animal images uniformly suggest loathesomeness, rapacity, or sheer brutishness. All this affords the clearest proof of an artist who knows how to reject. Consider this sequence: cold, Russia, winter, death, sickness, shadow, eclipse, darkness, mist. Of necessity, these images have been expressed here consecutively, as a chain. But their relations to one another would be represented much more accurately by a model, as of a molecular structure.

From a study of Webster's images one turns with renewed understanding to Woelfflin's statement of the baroque, 'The finite, the isolable, disappear'[72] And again, the passage cited on baroque portraiture is highly relevant here too: 'The very existence of the baroque figure . . . is bound to the other motives in the picture. Even the single portrait head is inextricably woven into the movement of the background, be it only the movement of light and dark.[73] 'The movement of light and dark': nothing could better describe the impression that Vittoria gives as we try to analyse her: 'Through darkenesse Diamonds spred their ritchest light' (III. ii. 305). Or 'the single portrait head . . . inextricably woven into the movement of the background': this defines all Websterian portraits. Bosola's portrait, a composite of images of animals, learning, and devils, represents and focuses the themes of natural evil and knowledge.

To conclude: a purely verbal study of Webster's images reveals the playwright's intellectual mastery of his thematic material. Such a study also reveals that the verbal images are planned

[72] Woelfflin, *Principles of Art History*, p. 161.
[73] Ibid., p. 169.

to interlock with the action, to a degree not paralleled in any of his contemporaries. The result is—to a reader—a structure of compelling emotional and intellectual effect. One awaits the day when the reader, as spectator, can agree that 'a great part of the grace of this . . . lay in Action.'

VI

CONCLUSION

To approach Webster from the viewpoint of the art historian is to gain fresh insight into his techniques and assumptions. One would like to use a convenient shorthand term, and refer to his style; this is, however, to court an ancient controversy, and one that I do not wish to enter upon here. The baroque style like all period styles may be considered as a Platonic idea, forming and moulding all the products of the baroque era; or as an abstraction, deduced from the characteristics of a number of works in that era. It is not necessary for me to adopt formally either of these positions, nor do I. My concern has been to identify certain technical characteristics that appear to be shared by Webster and his contemporaries in the visual arts, and I have indicated that these similarities come from similar causes. There, for the moment, we can leave the central problem of style. Considered purely as a set of technical characteristics, certain aspects of Webster's style are bound to strike the historian of the arts more forcibly than the historian of literature. It is an illumination, and a corrective to critical judgement, to study Webster at least initially from this viewpoint. Certain aspects then emerge prominently; they emphasize themselves as basic to any assessment of Webster's art; they link him to the movement of his times. They lead to the broad conclusion I suggested at the outset, that Webster is a prime example of baroque.

Those criteria for describing the baroque style—criteria widely accepted as useful by art historians—that I have applied to Webster, are met to a high degree in his two major tragedies. He is not, of course, unique in his expression of these criteria. He is unique, among his fellow dramatists, in his extreme pursuit of them. Webster is not, perhaps, more obviously 'sensational' than, say Marston, or Ford; but he lays down a barrage of manipulative devices that extend the concept. His plays are intensely, and variedly, sensational. Again, it is hardly possible to exceed the ironies of Tourneur; but Webster's ironies, culminating in *The Duchess of Malfi*, are as sustained, and more inventive. Any leading dramatist of the period knows how to leave questions unanswered about the main characters; the method is Shakespearean. None, I think, so aggressively asserts the problematic nature of 'character'. Outside the realms of hack dramaturgy, we nowhere find behaviour that oscillates so wildly, evidence that appears so contradictory, 'final' statements that are so disturbingly provisional. Webster has a profoundly baroque appreciation of the indefinability of the human essence; his portraiture is, and is meant to be, blurred. As for multiplicity in unity, there is no name that can be advanced to furnish a comparison. The density of Webster's verbal imagery is in itself unique; so is its tight interconnection with the events of the action. Together, figure-in-word and figure-in-action form a mode of construction that stands alone in the Jacobean drama. And these criteria, which I have described at some length in Webster, are of course accompanied by other general characteristics of the baroque, which are too broad and too obviously applicable to Webster to warrant painstaking study. One may name intense emotionality; extravagance of language and behaviour, bordering on the bizarre; a fascination with the intricacies of the human mind; a profound sense that man lives in a context of time, and death; as baroque characteristics that are also, and self-evidently, Webster's. All these characteristics stamp Webster as baroque. And they combine to assert that the drama of Webster is, in a word, theatrical. To reject the word is to reject the foundations of Webster's art.

Webster, then, is an extremist. And if we seek to penetrate beyond the characteristics of his art to the creating mind, we find that here, too, he seems designed to illustrate Zevedei Barbu's epitome of the baroque mind:

. . . the baroque is the expression at the cultural level of a specific mental structure resulting from the psycho-historical situation of the interregnum period. The implication of this is that there exists such a thing as a baroque mind which is the source of specific artistic techniques, specific attitudes to life, and a specific conception of man. In other words, the baroque can be spoken of in terms of a basic personality structure. Thus, irregularity and amplitude of forms, inner contradictions, the feeling of statelessness and of the fantastic are so many expressions of a personality structure with a low degree of integration.[74]

And again:

For a more adequate psychological understanding of this phenomenon we have to take into account, among other things, the fact that the baroque in visual art as well as the literary baroque arose towards the end of the interregnum period, that is to say, at a time when the anxiety created by the disintegration of the old world, of the old super-ego in particular, began to subside, and when the shape of the new world was well in sight. . . . The baroque expresses a state of inner contradiction and anarchy in the depth of human existence, and at the same time a daring and vigorous formative urge; . . .[75]

The idea that stylistic characteristics have a psycho-social determinant is not to be avoided. And Barbu's formulation of the 'baroque mind', if accepted, would do much to explain the problem of John Webster. Flamineo and Bosola, his central character-studies, embody perfectly the 'disintegration of the old world', together with the 'personality structure with a low degree of integration'. The questionings of *The Duchess of Malfi*, that supreme depiction of a universe without answers, provides an *interrogatio* that is in its way as emphatic as *Hamlet's*.[76] All values, in fact, are brought to the question by the author of *The White Devil* and *The Duchess of Malfi*, before being given a precarious resolution in 'integrity of life'. Granted the hypothesis of the baroque mind, there is a strong case for accepting Webster as a major instance of that mind in action.[77]

[74] Zevedei Barbu, *Problems of Historical Psychology* (Grove Press, New York, 1960), pp. 177–9.

[75] Ibid., p. 178.

[76] Cf. Harry Levin's reading of *Hamlet* in *The Question of Hamlet* (O.U.P., New York, 1959).

[77] A complementary—one need not say alternative—thesis is advanced by Baldini (op. cit., pp. 159–63). He suggests a direct relationship between Webster and the visual arts of the period, via the workshops of the Flemish painters in England that we know to have existed in the late Elizabethan and Jacobean periods. The suggestion is seductive; and certainly, if one had to indicate the painters whose work most recalls Webster, one would name Bosch and Breughel, together with their Flemish followers. But the materials for documenting such a relationship are far too tenuous, and I cannot find evidence to warrant an argument on direct-relationship lines. It does, however, appear as a legitimate possibility. See Ellis Waterhouse's remarks on the dynasties of De Critz and Gheeraerts, in *Painting in Britain 1530–1790* (Penguin, Harmondsworth, 1953), pp. 25–8. One should also note the efforts of Henry, during his brief life as Prince of Wales

But however much the concept of baroque helps us to understand Webster, it provides no automatic defence of his work. Since a period style is neutral, exponents of it may be good or bad. It is the use made of it that matters. Hence successful criticism of Webster, whether adverse or favourable, should be directed towards the connections between his techniques and purposes. There is much in Webster that seems to call, at first, for purely technical assessment. The relationship of one scene to another, say, or the propriety of a device to the genre, are matters that may be discussed in a fairly limited way. But sooner or later one must move from the techniques to the purposes, or to the view of humanity that the play projects. The inconsistent and self-contradictory behaviour of the main characters dramatizes the problems of essence and identity, problems very acutely analysed in *The Duchess of Malfi*. Irony, the key to so much of Webster's work, is at bottom an apprehension of man as a being dominated by time and death. And always the issue of sensationalism remains to focus the argument. Sensationalism is not a matter that can be satisfyingly discussed in terms of a specific episode or device. It demands an assessment of the mind behind the device. If one feels that the sensational has become the end of the dramatic enterprise, or that the playwright has become fascinated by the minutiae of his technical accomplishment, then one is entitled to condemn him. Decadence is at least partially definable as the supremacy of form over content. But if one feels that the dramatist is deploying his effects to a legitimate purpose, then one accepts the means he has chosen. Gratuitous theatricality, impact in a moral void, is one thing. A society created by the dramatist, bearing the impress of consistency and truth, and presented as powerfully as possible, is another.

What can guide us in arriving at a judgement on Webster's purposes, as distinct from his allowed mastery of psychology, situation, and poetry? There is little point in analysing the subject matter of his plays. That, as Canon Kingsley correctly indicated, is merely a catalogue of crime. And naturally, no

---

(1610–12) to import an Italian aesthetics into the English Court and English art. Webster may well have known, and appreciated, something of what Henry was trying to do. But he does not take the opportunity to elaborate on this aspect of Henry's life in 'A Monumental Columne', though there is a reference to 'yong, grave *Mecaenas* of the noble arts'. Lucas, iii. 271, line 276.

critic can seriously argue that because the evil-doers are killed off in Act V, this demonstrates the soundness of the playwright's principles. That is an argument one associates with those responsible for a more than usually lurid crime series on television. But beneath the subject matter, which is crime, there emerges in Webster something quite distinct: a profound sense of evil. And against evil stands its adversary and judge: the Law. The intense concern with the issues of evil and the Law, a concern detectable throughout the major work of Webster, is that of a moralist. I do not argue that Webster was more moralist than dramatist: they are not mutually exclusive terms. It is soundest to see him as a dramatist profoundly involved in moral issues, one who realizes that drama, like debate, is a form well suited to the projection of moral issues. Those issues do not yield an easy 'moral'. They are nevertheless at the heart of Webster's drama. It is this that underwrites his work, and that constitutes the proper defence to the charge of sensationalism.

Our analysis, then, proceeds no further on stylistic matters. It is now necessary to examine the nature and the detail of the moral issues I have indicated. To do that, one turns to the content of Webster's drama.

Part Two

THEMES

I

INTRODUCTION

The ends-means equation must dominate a discussion of Webster's art. The first necessity of baroque is that the audience should be gripped, excited, moved. But major art rests on foundations that remain valid after the turbulence of the immediate emotions has died. And these foundations must include the content—I do not mean, the subject matter—of the drama. That can afford an answer to the question: what are the positive concerns of the playwright? What, even more simply, are his plays about?

The obvious answer is that the *sententiae* constitute the moral concerns of the plays. These are the points where the action halts, the text leaps into inverted commas, and a moral generalization is enunciated on the situation of the characters. Naturally, most of the action is completely opposed to the drift of the *sententiae*, and Ian Jack sees in this the fundamental flaw of Webster:

. . . this background of moral doctrine has nothing to do with the action of the plays: so far from growing out of the action, it has all the marks of having been superimposed by the poet in a cooler, less creative mood than that in which the Duchess and Flamineo had their birth. There is no correspondence between the axioms and the life represented in the drama. This dissociation is the fundamental flaw in Webster.[1]

The dissociation is certainly a fundamental fact of Webster; but it prefers no charge against the playwright. It is obviously true that 'There is no correspondence between the axioms and the life represented in the drama'. This is on a par with writing: 'There is no correspondence between Clytemnestra's action in killing Agamemnon and the views expressed by the chorus.' For this is what the *sententiae* amount to. They fulfil, in diffused form, the function of the chorus; and the practice of Euripides (especially)

[1] Ian Jack, 'The Case of John Webster', *Scrutiny*, xvi (1949), 39.

and Sophocles had demonstrated that the choric viewpoint, though an important one, is not final and definitive. And the drama consists essentially of the gap between the choric morality and the actions of the principal characters. Webster himself, *in propria persona*, had lamented that he could not include in his play 'the sententious Chorus . . . the passionate and weighty Nuntius',[2] but found the true correlative of the chorus. His *sententiae* outline a body of conventional moral wisdom, to which his characters refer, but to which they cannot adhere. Such a situation is not much unlike life itself. It is curious that Webster should be censured for a most original dramatic procedure: that is, the development of the old chorus not into a self-contained unit of expression (Enobarbus, Thersites) but as a part of the character's mind. As a depiction of a disintegrating world order, this procedure deserves some recognition in the twentieth century.

The *sententiae* do not, in themselves, tell us what the plays are about. A broad indication, of a sort, is supplied by the plots. The plots of Webster's three plays, taken alone, afford inadequate but not misleading statements of his intentions. *The White Devil* is essentially a pattern of evil-doers and of retribution; *The Duchess of Malfi* reveals humanity, rather than evil-doers, gripped by a malevolent or indifferent fate; *The Devil's Law-Case* is a story of wrong unpunished. Such are the stories, and such the essences of his three plays. But to demonstrate fully the playwright's design one must look elsewhere.

The concerns of Webster are located in the imagery of his plays. The imagery is the basic content of his work; it reveals the primary symbols through which Webster's imagination expresses itself. It is not solely a matter of verbal imagery; as we have seen, the interconnections of action, character, and words make all partial analyses highly provisional. But a study must be based on the words of the text. These texts are massive growths of imagery; it would be misleading to speak of a 'pattern of imagery' as a sort of necklace of verbal brilliants that rest on the otherwise unadorned body of the play. On the contrary, *The White Devil* and *The Duchess of Malfi* would have virtually no text left were one to remove the imagery. The motifs that can be discerned here offer the best indications of Webster's concerns.

The method for establishing image themes, as developed by

---

[2] Webster's 'To the Reader' of *The White Devil*. Lucas, i. 107.

Caroline Spurgeon, Wilson Knight, and Wolfgang Clemen, lends itself to varying emphases but in essence remains constant. Two stages are necessary: first, a descriptive analysis, by subject matter, of the play's images; second, a reclassification of the images that brings together images from various groups into one thematic category. The second stage of the analysis concentrates on the images that seem to play a special and functional part in the movement of the play. Usually the analyst can obtain certain clues, apart from his own judgement, in locating these special images. One is likely to find, on a comparison with other plays by contemporary dramatists, or with other plays by the same dramatist, that certain motifs leap into prominence. Thus Caroline Spurgeon found a major significance in some ten images of clothing in *Macbeth*.[3] Webster, however, usually makes his thematic points through a considerable weight of iterative imagery. They give the impression (which is supported by his own admission of being a slow worker) of being deployed in accordance with a conscious intellectual design.

A primary classification of Webster's images reveals his fascination with certain areas of subject matter.[4] Images of animals and disease figure very largely in all three of his plays. *The White Devil* and *The Duchess of Malfi* draw heavily, in addition, on images that embody the opposition of appearance and reality. Passing from images, defined strictly, to words significantly repeated in the two tragedies, one finds many references to devils and to witches; and in the Machiavellian group, to 'great men', 'princes', 'politic', and 'policy'. These are the data which a secondary classification must interpret. All of these images and words are subsumed in a single theme, that of evil. Evidently, this theme is embodied in the actions of the leading characters. His plays are saturated with a consciousness of human evil.

There is a further area of subject matter, treated in all three plays, which points towards the other grand theme that dominates the imagination of Webster. It is the Law. Numerically far fewer than those embodying the theme of evil, images of the Law occur at critical points in *The White Devil* and *The Duchess of Malfi*. (The Law is, of course, the substance of the plot itself in *The Devil's Law-Case*, and the dialogue there contains a multitude of literal references in addition to certain metaphors.) The

[3] Spurgeon, op. cit., pp. 324–7.   [4] See Part I, note 64.

idea of the Law is supported by a number of verbal counters that present aspects of the same concept: justice, revenge, service, payment, reward. Moreover, an important aspect of the Law—retribution—is present in the many images of storm in the two tragedies. Finally, we can note that the trial scene is the theatrical centre of *The White Devil* and *The Devil's Law-Case*, and a miniature trial (the dialogue of Ferdinand and Bosola) is correspondingly placed (iv. ii) in *The Duchess of Malfi*. The images of the Law, together with its associated terms, stand for the mechanisms whereby man governs himself—and by which the universe governs him. They constitute one of the two major themes that dominate Webster's imagination. While other themes of importance exist in his plays—most notably, the theme of knowledge in *The Duchess of Malfi*—only these themes figure largely in all three plays.

The relationship between evil and the Law is the intellectual tension that grips *The White Devil*, *The Duchess of Malfi*, and *The Devil's Law-Case*. The resolution of that tension is the main concern of each play; for while human evil may be a constant, the Law is not. It is presented in turn as a simple retributive mechanism that punishes wrongdoers, as the ineluctable fate that awaits a sinful humanity, and as a moral and ethical code of human conduct—a central, albeit unfulfilled, ideal.

The thematic concerns of this playwright do, however, raise criticisms of a quite different order from those I have considered earlier. The mass of imagery of which each tragedy is composed invites, to my mind, two objections that have not been urged against Webster in the past. They can conveniently be considered at this point. First, it may be said that the sheer bulk of the imagery is altogether too much strain upon the audience. The ornamentation of a baroque façade is one thing; the spectator has no fixed time in which to absorb the implications of the manifold detail. The dense imagery of a Webster play is a different matter, since the audience must be supposed to be capable of assimilating it without preparation and within a given time-limit. It is true that *The Duchess of Malfi* is slightly lighter in texture than *The White Devil*, and *The Devil's Law-Case* contains a much smaller quantity of imagery than the tragedies. Perhaps Webster had listened to the complaint that his audience needed much more non-metaphoric dialogue on which to 'rest' their minds. Even if one allows for heavy cuts in performance, one is still left with a residual play of high metaphorical content. This 'overloading' of the audience's mind is undoubtedly a deliberate objective of Webster's art; it complements his other varieties of sensationalism. But in practice the two tragedies must always pose formidable problems of assimilation. I think it a telling charge to level against Webster's stagecraft.

The second objection lying in wait for the expounder of themes is that the plays are too literary and schematic. The patterns of imagery may be so obtrusive as to impair the effectiveness of the plays in performance, since a play is in the first instance a record of human activity, not an aggregation of symbols conveniently broken down into lines of dialogue. Either the playwright, or the critic, is too schematic; on one of these horns the critic can be gored. The critic must take his chance, but can plead that his *schema* is an abstraction, an aid to interpretation, not a model that represents formally the play experience. The critic's *schema* does not correspond to the play in the same way that a map does to the terrain. Webster's *schema* requires careful identification. I believe that Webster worked, very slowly and deliberately, towards a definite intellectual objective; and that he excluded from his work ideas and material that might conflict with that design. The ideas that constitute his intellectual objective are constantly re-embodied in the words and actions of his characters. And the implications and associations of those words are, as I have shown (page 67), highly restrictive in value. It sounds like a formula for dead theatre. How, then, can we account for the continuing life of Webster on stage? The answer, I suggest, is that the play structure contains much more than the ideas that may be abstracted. The characters of a Webster play obstinately maintain a life of their own; they assert it against the very text.

That this is possible, the themes of their nature admit. For evil and the Law have quite different implications for the theatre. The Law is readily embodied in action; and since the tragedies are much concerned with reward (Flamineo and Bosola) and punishment (almost all the leading characters) the concept can readily be elaborated in a fairly programmatic way, one that leaves untouched the separate questions of character and psychology. But Webster's emphasis on the evil of his stage society does not exclude counter-suggestions. Flamineo and Bosola are not invulnerable to the occasional impulse of decency; Brachiano dies trying to shield 'that good woman', Vittoria, from poison; Lodovico urges his master not to expose himself to danger; Ferdinand is the wreck of a prince, a part invariably allotted to an actor of distinction; the marble façade of the Cardinal cracks at the last. As with character, so with the body. I record later that the body is invariably alluded to as the symbol of corruption and mortality. It is one of the most consistent correspondences that Webster employs. But the stage actors are, to appearances, very far from corrupt. The Duchess and Vittoria are beautiful women; Brachiano has none of the physical grossness of his historical source (a pointer, this, to Webster's intentions); Antonio must be a pretty enough fellow, and Julia finds plenty to admire in Bosola.[5] Certainly, all this may be held to embody the appearance-reality opposition in a rather schematic form. But its effect on the audience must be an impression of complexity, of opposed tendencies and suggestions. And that impression, naturally, is heightened by the blurring and inconsistency of character that I have already considered. In brief, the intellectual concerns of Webster seem to me perfectly compatible with the needs of the theatre.

[5] Naturally, the physical beauty of the actors need not, in practice, exclude a strong suggestion of corruption and animality. Piero Gherardi's designs for the National Theatre production (1969) communicated this idea in original fashion. The set was a huge, honey-coloured wall: 'It is a wall as it might be perceived by insects or small reptiles: toads, perhaps, or grasshoppers or drones.' (Benedict Nightingale, reviewing the play in the *New Statesman*, 21 November 1969.) The costumes elaborated the insect metaphor, itself taking up Brooke's view of the characters as 'writhing grubs in an immense night'. The metaphorical point was well taken by a number of critics. Especially worthy of study, in addition to the *New Statesman* review cited above, are Ronald Bryden's review in the *Observer* (14 November) and Hilary Spurling's in the *Spectator* (22 November).

1. Caravaggio: *The Flagellation of Christ*. Naples, S. Domenico Maggiore, 1606–1607

2. Caravaggio: *The Beheading of S. John the Baptist*. Valetta, Cathedral, 1607–1608

3. Rembrandt: *The Blinding of Samson*. Frankfurt-am-Main, Städelsches Kunstinstitut, 1636

4. Antonio d'Enrico, il Tanzio: *David and Goliath*. Varallo, Pinacoteca, after 1620

5. Guercino: *Aurora*. Rome, Ceiling to the Villa Ludovisi, 1623

6. Gaulli: *The Adoration of the Name of Jesus*. Rome, Ceiling of the nave of the Church of Gesù

7. Parmigianino: *Self-Portrait*. Vienna, Kunsthistorisches Museum, 1524

8. Johann Heinrich Keller: *Knorpelsgroteske*. c. 1680

9. Jacques Callot:
   From the *Sketchbooks*

10. Jacques Callot: *Gobbi*. 1616

11. Bernini: *Caricature of Cardinal Scipio Borghese*. Rome, Biblioteca Corsini

12. Van Dyck: *The Abbé Scaglia*. Collection of Lord Camrose, 1634

13. Rembrandt: *Self-Portrait*. Vienna, Kunsthistorisches Museum, c. 1657

II

THE WHITE DEVIL

1. EVIL

(a) Animal

There are, as Miss Bradbrook remarks, over 100 animal references in *The White Devil*.[6] She lists over thirty in Act V alone. It is an interminable bestiary, which I spare the reader here. Two animals stand out: the wolf and the dog. The wolf, indeed, virtually begins the play:

> Your woolfe no longer seemes to be a woolfe
> Then when shees hungry.
>
> (ɪ. i. 8–9)

This is of 'great men': the image is a focus for the predator in mankind—and womankind:

> Woman to man
> Is either a God or a wolfe.
>
> (ɪv. ii. 92–3)

cries Brachiano, in his agony of disillusion. And at the last it is the wolf, 'that's foe to man', which Brachiano fears; his dying vision is of a grave where

> the hoarse wolfe
> Sents not they carion.
>
> (v. iii. 33–4)

The wolf is a symbol of ferocity and unquiet, opposed to man and yet of man. It is a symbol of intense yet limited range, and on that account perhaps of less interest than the dog. For the dog is associated with a wide range of qualities, not least its virtues. But of these, no hint is given. The dog images convey the ideas of cowardice, loathesomeness, abjectness; a fair specimen is

---

[6] Bradbrook, op. cit., p. 194.

> *Lodovico.*   And thou shalt die like a poore rogue.
> *Gasparo.*   And stinke
>   Like a dead flie-blowne dog.
>
> (v. iii. 167–8)

It is Brachiano's fate to hear these lines on his deathbed—he, who had once scorned his enemies as 'dogs'. The irony accords well with an aspect of the play's dialogue that is properly termed cynical. The chief mouthpiece for these images is Flamineo; and when he says, 'Ile unkennell one example more for thee' (v. i. 166–7) it is clear that cynical, in both the derivative and the customary sense, is the correct adjective for much of the play's substance.

It is already plain that the animal images serve to comment on the brutish in man. The world of the animal parallels, seems almost to fuse with, the world of man. The technique recalls *King Lear*, even if the comparison between animal and man has a much longer parentage. And here, just as in Shakespeare, the animals express a sexual appetence that yields a sustained shudder at the copulation of man and woman: Flamineo, no man to provide an ounce of civet to sweeten the imagination, is the one to point the connection:

> Women are caught as you take Tortoises,
> Shee must bee turn'd on her backe.
>
> (iv. ii. 154–5)

> Young Leverets stand not long; and womens anger
> Should, like their flight, procure a little sport;
> A full crie for a quarter of an hower;
> And then bee put to th' dead quat.
>
> (iv. ii. 162–5)

Further examples could be accumulated *ad nauseam*. Stag, tortoise, leveret, dog, ferret, hare, wild duck, silkworm—each of these animals is used to illustrate the sexual proclivities of the principals. Many of these analogies are Flamineo's; and that choric voice seems to fix the idea of sex as a copulation. Small wonder that Brooke was impelled to write of 'writhing grubs in an immense night',[7] and Bogard of the Websterian 'jungle'.[8]

It is impossible to resist the conclusion that Webster had

---

[7] Brooke, op. cit., p. 158.   [8] Bogard, op. cit., p. 79.

assimilated much of *King Lear*, and was developing the animal imagery for the same dramatic purpose.[9] Bradley, writing of *King Lear*, uses terms that could be applied to *The White Devil* without the least modification:

This mode of thought is responsible, lastly, for a very striking characteristic of *King Lear*—one in which it has no parallel except *Timon*—the incessant references to the lower animals and man's likeness to them. These references are scattered broadcast through the whole play, as though Shakespeare's mind were so busy with the subject that he could hardly write a page without some allusion to it.[10]

It is not merely a matter of quantity. Webster finds in the subject what Shakespeare found in it: the bestiality of beasts, and their affinities with the bestiality of man.

As we read, the souls of all the beasts in turn seem to us to have entered into the bodies of these mortals; horrible in their venom, savagery, lust, deceitfulness, sloth, cruelty, filthiness; miserable in their feebleness, nakedness, defencelessness, blindness; and man, 'consider him well', is even what they are.[11]

The ideas designated by Bradley are repeated by Webster, within a narrower compass. The qualities suggested by the animals of *The White Devil* are threefold: rapacity, loathesomeness, sexual appetence. It is a sustained metaphorical comment, of singular intensity, on the world of the play.

(b) Disease

Caroline Spurgeon, dealing with the atmosphere of *Hamlet*, had this to say: '[it] is partly due to the number of images of sickness, disease, or blemish of the body, in the play, and we discover that the idea of an ulcer or tumour, as descriptive of the unwholesome condition of Denmark, is, on the whole, the dominating one.'[12] This statement, just and penetrating as it undoubtedly is,

[9] It is possible that Webster had learned something from Marston's (say) handling of animal and disease imagery. But it is clear that he had studied *King Lear* closely. Aside from the general question of Webster's debt to Shakespeare, R. W. Dent has noted (in *John Webster's Borrowing*) a number of verbal borrowings from *King Lear*. And there is a broad structural similarity between *King Lear* and *The Duchess of Malfi*, two tragedies of suffering.

[10] A. C. Bradley, *Shakespearean Tragedy* (Macmillan, London, 1957), p. 218.

[11] Ibid.

[12] Spurgeon, op. cit., p. 316.

was made on the basis of twenty images concerned with sickness and medicine; twenty out of 279, a little over 7 per cent. I find that in *The White Devil* sixty-six images, in all, treat of sickness and corruption, physic and physicians; that is, 13 per cent out of some 500. This is an astonishing figure. If *Hamlet* is a play concerned with disease, *The White Devil* is a play obsessed with it. The images deal many times, in a general way, with plague, sickness, poison, and putrefaction; specifically they name vomiting, jaundice, fits, fevers, piles, palsy, syphilis, bee-stings, ulcer, abscess, halitosis, cancer, ague, falling-sickness, and the common cold; fractures, purgatives and emetics, plasters, stitches, crutches, and pills. Here is the clearest evidence of a mind continuously running on disease, continuously seeking to underscore the action in terms of medical imagery. Through the medium of these images Webster makes, in my judgement, his most deeply felt comment on the nature of mortality and of mankind's tragedy.

To begin with generalities: it is clear on the most superficial reading of the play that the action is constantly compared with the processes of disease and corruption. The main origin of these metaphors is seen to be Court life, an endlessly corrupting milieu of materialism and self-seeking. (Flamineo's motivation speech, I. ii. 308–25, makes the connection clear.) The nature of this corruption is epitomized in Flamineo's 'Theres nothing so holie but mony will corrupt and putrifie it, like vittell under the line' (III. iii. 24–5). Physical diseases figure the moral corruption that stems from the Court. So much is general, and obvious. But a deeper significance emerges from the variety singled out for pre-eminence. One disease only receives frequent allusion in *The White Devil*: syphilis. I have noticed six clear-cut allusions, and may well have missed others buried in the *doubles entendres* of the text. All but one refer to Brachiano: there are two allusions to his 'moulting', and his own prophetic outcry

> Oh, I could bee mad,
> Prevent the curst disease shee'l bring mee to;
> And teare my haire off.
>
> (IV. ii. 47–9)

How are we to read these allusions? Similar images are of course to be found in a multitude of contemporary plays. But it would be superficial to write them off as **routine** examples of Jacobean bawdry. The syphilis idea bridges two major themes. Two points stand out. The venereal references blend with the animal images; they stress the point—which the audience has already well digested—that man, 'the paragon of animals', is often enough more animal than paragon. Moreover, such references link with the idea of reward and punishment. For this disease is not merely an act of God; it is a consequence of specific, and in Webster's code sinful, human acts. The retribution for this sin is definite, and horrific. The quotations refer to Brachiano and his liaison with Vittoria. As it happens, he does not suffer from the disease, but his actual fate closely parallels its course. He is rotted not by disease, but by poison; he tears off, not his hair, but his beaver. Brachiano's death is virtually a figure-in-action; and the syphilis images are thus a small but functional part of the play's structure.

Vittoria herself is presented as a disease. Her corrupting potential is stressed by Monticelso throughout the trial scene. There, in addition, her sin is seen as an ulcer; the lawyer thunders against her

> Exorbitant sinnes must have exulceration.
>
> (III. ii. 37)

There is here a question of meaning. Lucas glosses the line '. . . must involve, inflame exasperation'.[13] In J. R. Brown's edition occurs the note: 'Leech suggests that the lawyer means, vaguely, "extirpation".'[14] I think this far more likely. The lawyer seems to be saying that the ulcer must be cut out. Assuming this to be the meaning, it becomes a parody of an essential truth. The judgement is ironically reinforced by Vittoria herself:

> I had a limbe corrupted to an ulcer,
> But I have cut it off; and now Ile go
> Weeping to heaven on crutches.
>
> (IV. ii. 122–4)

The ulcer identifies Vittoria. All turns on her; the action stems from her liaison with Brachiano, a joint sin seen as a disease. She is the focus of the theme of moral disease, and of Webster's deeper meaning. And any assessment of that meaning must account for Vittoria's ambiguous dying words:

---

[13] Lucas, i. 229.
[14] Brown, *The White Devil*, p. 67.

> O my greatest sinne lay in my blood.
>
> (v. vi. 240)

If we pursue the disease metaphor towards cure, we find a consistent *schema*. Physic, in the imagery of *The White Devil*, never takes on the connotations of healing, balm, and recovery. It is at best unpleasant, at worst deadly. Frequently it is presented as purgative: 'we now, like the partridge,/Purge the disease with lawrell' (v. iii. 278–9). 'Pills' are invariably linked with death: 'I decerne poison /Under your guilded pils' (iii. ii. 198–9). Such passages find their apotheosis in the final scene:

> *Flamineo.* And ô contemtible Physike! that dost take
> So long a study, onely to preserve
> So short a life, I take my leave of thee.
> These are two cupping-glasses, that shall draw
> All my infected bloud out—
>
> (v. vi. 102–6)

The dramatist shows his hand clearly via the technique of truth parodied (Flamineo is play-acting here). Physic is useless; blood must be drawn, for death is the only cure when the blood is infected. The matter resolves itself into this progression: sin is a disease; the disease lies in the blood; the only cure is blood-letting, which is death.

The metaphor extends, finally, to the physicians. These are no mere incidental props, but are fully integrated with the play's structure. Since they have virtually no individual characteristics, they are of a different order from the major characters. Flamineo refuses to be schematized; the physicians, as I judge, owe their stage existence to the *schema*. A 'doctor' is employed by Brachiano to poison his Duchess, an office which that genial disciple of Hippocrates faithfully discharges. And the physicians whom Brachiano calls upon in his death-agony are powerless. Brachiano's comment is upon the species, not the individual representative:

> Most corrupted pollitick hangman!
> You kill without booke; but your art to save
> Failes you as oft, as great mens needy friends.
>
> (v. iii. 21–3)

It is a statement extended through the comparable term 'apothecary'. There is no clear-cut distinction between the functions of

doctor and apothecary. So it is consistent that Brachiano's ren-
dezvous with Vittoria should take place in an apothecary's
summer-house (iii. ii. 202), that she should be compared to a
'Poticaries shop' of poisons (iii. ii. 109), and that Brachiano
should die with 'develish potticarie stuffe' melting in his brains
(v. iii. 164–5). It is a pure irony for Brachiano to address
Vittoria as a 'sweet Phisition' (i. ii. 199); later he is to curse her
for the 'curst disease shee'l bring mee to' (iv. ii. 48). The
essence of the physician's trade is realized most fully, perhaps,
in these two views of him:

> *Flamineo.* . . . some Surgeon's house at Venice, built upon the
> Pox as well as on piles . . .
>
> (iii. iii. 8–9)

> *Monticelso.* [Of whores] They are worse
> Worse then dead bodies, which are beg'd at gallowes
> And wrought upon by surgeons' to teach man
> Wherin hee is imperfect.
>
> (iii. ii. 99–102)

There it is: a trade built on the diseases of man, commanding
at best a front view of the imperfections of man. The progression
is complete. To live is to sin; sin, like life generally, is a disease;
the cure is death only; the physicians are rogues. In Webster's
attitude towards physicians can be seen perhaps the profoundest
proof of his pessimism. They are, or could be, the one symbol of
hope in a diseased world. And they are worthless; the hope is
delusory.

The sum of the many images of animals and disease is a statement of unmistakable weight. It is not an absolute condemnation
of the human race; just as Cordelia, Kent, Albany, and Edgar are
the major saving clauses in *King Lear*, so are Cornelia, Marcello,
Giovanni, and Isabella in *The White Devil*. But there is an insistent metaphorical suggestion that animals provide appropriate
emblems for the human race, and that the over-all characteristic
of humanity is corruption. Physical disease figures a moral sickness.

(c) *Appearance/Reality and Machiavellianism*

Other metaphors for humanity announce the theme of evil much
more explicitly. Evil is consistently located in the antithesis of

appearance and reality. Over a score of images embody this antithesis, a very strong collective verdict on the nature of evil. The most important is the emblematic title of the play, on which Lucas's gloss reads: 'A devil disguised under a fair outside'.[15] In the Trial scene, Monticelso delivers what is virtually a dramatized sermon on this text. Thus, a cosmetics image reveals her falsity:

> I shall bee playner with you, and paint out
> Your folies in more naturall red and white
> Then that upon your cheeke.
>
> (III. ii. 54–6)

An apple from Sodom and Gomorrah symbolizes her moral state (III. ii. 65–70), as do three references to counterfeiting. Monticelso's summing up is

> if the devill
> Did ever take good shape behold his picture.
>
> (III. ii. 224–5)

Evidently, there exists a number of images presenting Vittoria's evil in appearance-reality terms. But they are not exclusive to her. The whole play is studded with such images, which provide a context for all the leading characters (who, by definition, are the evil-doers). The idea is present, for instance, in 'painted comforts' (I. i. 50), in Lodovico's

> I have seene some ready to be executed
> Give pleasant lookes, and money, and growne familiar
> With the knave hangman—
>
> (I. i. 53–5)

and in Flamineo's

> "But seas doe laugh, shew white, when Rocks are neere.
>
> (v. vi. 251)

Frequently the idea is linked with the activities of 'great men', 'politicians', i.e. the Machiavellians.[16] Thus, Flamineo has

[15] Lucas, i. 193.

[16] See Mario Praz, 'Machiavelli and the Elizabethans', *Proceedings of the British Academy*, xiv (1928), 49–97. The impact of Machiavelli on contemporary thought in England is studied in Felix Raab's *The English Face of Machiavelli* (Routledge and Kegan Paul, London, 1964). He shows that Machiavelli was not simply a stereotype of evil. Rather, Machiavelli became the focus of a continuing debate; and the

> if you will be merry
> Do it i'th like posture, as if some great man
> Sate while his enemy were executed:
> Though it be very letchery unto thee,
> Do't with a crabbed Politicians face.
>
> (III. iii. 100–4)

and notes it as characteristic of the 'rare trickes of a Machivillian' (v. iii. 196). But the antithesis of seeming and being takes on a different implication with Lodovico's

> fine imbrodered bottles,
> And perfumes
> Equally mortall with a winter plague.
>
> (v. iii. 159–61)

The appearance-reality opposition is now merged with the transience of all earthly glories. It is a notion fixed by Flamineo's *sententia* (one that is repeated verbatim in *The Duchess of Malfi*):

> Glories, like glow-wormes, afarre off shine bright
> But lookt to neare, have neither heat nor light.
>
> (v. i. 38–9)

Broadly speaking, I discern three related ideas in these images. Vittoria is evil because she is unlike her fair exterior. The counterfeit, Dead Sea fruit images symbolize her moral state, quite apart from her actions. It is a matter of being. Next, the actions of the Machiavellians (a term which Webster uses loosely, together with 'great men', to cover most Court dwellers) are seen as evil because they are oblique, indirect, treacherous. Though there is only one direct reference to Machiavelli in the play, and one quotation,

> Foole! Princes give rewards with their owne hands,
> But death or punishment by the handes of others.
>
> (v. vi. 189–90)

Machiavellianism permeates the atmosphere of *The White Devil*, through the many references to 'Princes', 'politicians', 'politic',

---

references to him reveal a tension between the traditional theological outlook and Machiavellian secularism. The growth of the secular outlook on political affairs is well illustrated in Henry Wright's remarkable *The First Part of the Disquisition of Truth concerning Political Affairs* (1616). Published two years after *The Duchess of Malfi*, this work accepted an overtly secular viewpoint. Yet it seems to have appeared without controversy.

and 'great men'. Finally, the concept takes on a new implication with the opposition between terrestrial glories and mortality. For this aspect of Webster's mind, 'satiric' is too narrow. 'He saw the skull beneath the skin' remains the most telling judgement.

Plainly, the opposition of appearance and reality conveys an apprehension of evil. Virtually no counter-statement exists in the imagery of this play; Marcello, Isabella, and Cornelia are as inadequate in imagery as in action. However, as Webster's thinking on this matter appears to be consistent, one can reasonably quote from *The Duchess of Malfi* and *The Devil's Law-Case*. The Duchess identifies

> the path
> Of simple vertue, which was never made
> To seeme the thing it is not . . .
> (I. i. 512–14)

And the same value is expressed by Leonora:

> There is then a heavenly beautie in't, the Soule
> Mooves in the Superficies.
> (I. i. 191–2)

These are useful as explicit statements of the idea. Beauty (a word with moral rather than aesthetic implications here) exists when there is no opposition between a fair surface and the inner reality.

(d) Devils and Witches

Evil becomes most explicit in the references to devils and witches that provide a strong and reiterated identification of the characters. 'Devil' occurs thirty-three times, 'witch' three times, and 'conjure' four. 'Devil' does not provide a sharp theological focus, but is used broadly, as an indicator of evil.

One can legitimately relate the few witchcraft images to the macabre, grotesque tone that Webster loves to evoke; as

> *Flamineo*   in stead of looking glasses
> To set ones face each morning by a sawcer
> Of a witches congealed blood.
> (III. iii. 84–6)

and III. i. 40–41. But the witchcraft idea merges, via conjuring, with devilry. The terms converge in

Monticelso.   And some there are which call it my blacke booke:
Well may the title hold: for though it teach not
The Art of conjuring, yet in it lurke
The names of many devils.
                                                (IV. i. 35–8)

'Devil' is applied consistently to all the leading characters. Such
references are divided equally between those that speak of *a* devil,
and *the* Devil. Webster uses the terms interchangeably and in-
differently.[17] This suggests a looseness of approach that emerges
clearly in a further association, that of 'devils' with 'furies':

Monticelso.   And so I leave thee
With all the Furies hanging bout thy necke,
Till by thy penitence thou remove this evill,
In conjuring from thy breast this cruell Devill.
                                                (IV. iii. 127–30)

Nor is this an isolated instance; apart from v. vi. 137–8, Lodovico
speaks of the 'three furies found in spacious hell' (IV. iii. 154).

All, then, are possessed by a devil; all are, to that extent, evil;
it is a ground-swell against our sympathies for Vittoria and, say,
Brachiano in his death scene. However, the rather indiscriminate
association of the devil, a devil, possession by a devil, witches,
conjuring, and furies does not suggest a hard core of theological
meaning here. Rather, it instances the characteristic Renaissance
eclecticism in theological matters.[18] Generally, these devil references recall *Dr Faustus*, and they look back beyond Marlowe
to the morality plays. *The White Devil* manifests something of
the same confrontation between good and evil as in *Dr Faustus*,
the role of the good angels being taken over by Antonelli and the
rest, while the remaining characters are presented as deeply
under the spell of devils. (Yet, though the bones show plainly,
the uses to which Webster puts the old tradition are striking. The
tradition is emphasized when Flamineo depicts Brachiano as clad

[17] See v. iii. 150–4.
[18] Jonson's 'Epitaph on Salomon Pavy', for example (vol. viii, p. 77 of Herford
and Simpson's edition) contains within the space of a few lines several references to
the Fates and to Heaven. After

As, sooth, the *Parcae* thought him one,
He plai'd so truely,

the poem ends

Heaven vowes to keepe him.

in his livery of flames, waited on by forty devils in hell. But the same passage reveals Flamineo, the professional careerist, ready to shake his dead master's hand in hell—when there is no profit to be gained from it.) And this is reinforced by the strong suggestion, already mentioned (see page 41) of the devilish parodies of marriage, confession, and extreme unction.

A very considerable part of the language of *The White Devil* is impregnated with the suggestion of evil. The many animal references provide an insistent metaphor for the human race; its inner corruption is signalled by the images of sickness and poison; the appearance-reality images point to evil in being, and evil in action; evil in the community is identified with the Machiavellians and Court dwellers; finally, the devil references take the theme almost out of the realm of metaphor, and identify the main characters as agents of evil. And this mass of statement and suggestion is reinforced by many other references that need only be alluded to here—the images of death and winter, and the oft-repeated 'black', virtually the only colour term employed in *The White Devil*. Taken together, these manifold images and references amount to a vast apprehension of human evil. One can readily understand how Lord David Cecil can write: 'His theology is Calvinistic. The world as seen by him is, of its nature, incurably corrupt.'[19] The point is accepted more cautiously by Clifford Leech, who writes of the 'Calvinist tinge' of Webster, and of his 'apparently unconscious acceptance of the doctrine of election'.[20] The sense of evil is so powerful in *The White Devil* that it may appear reasonable to accept 'Calvinist' as a way of describing this feeling.[21]

Yet the impulse to label Webster as a Calvinist should be checked. All religious matter in drama can be considered under two heads. First, there may be a series of religious references which, allied to the actions and fates of the characters, seems to present a coherent doctrine or viewpoint. This doctrine may be assumed to be shared by the dramatist. Second, there may be a mere accumulation of religious allusions, however powerfully

[19] Lord David Cecil, *Poets and Storytellers* (Longmans, London, 1949), p. 30.
[20] Clifford Leech, *John Webster* (Hogarth Press, London, 1951), pp. 60, 56.
[21] For a statement of the influence of Calvinism on the Jacobeans, see Michael H. Higgins, 'The Influence of Calvinistic Thought in Tourneur's *Atheist's Tragedy*', *Review of English Studies*, xix (1943), 255–62.

these may be shaded for certain dramatic effects. Here the play-wright is making use of theology, not disseminating it. In general, the enterprise of demonstrating this distinction runs into severe difficulties, once the safer varieties of homiletic drama are left behind. References of a vaguely religious nature occur readily in drama, most especially in tragedy. 'Good', 'bad', 'fate', 'freedom' are the common counters of existence, let alone drama. One easily acquires a mass of such terms. But constructing with them a theological cantilever supporting an entire play is something else again. It calls for a certain critical agility, allied to a single-mindedness that can border upon obsession. A fair instance of the problem is *The Merchant of Venice*. The Trial scene undoubtedly projects a very strong sense of religious values, of guilt/damnation versus justice/mercy. The religious overtones intensify our experience of the scene. Yet there has been little support for the contention that *The Merchant of Venice* is, over all, an allegory.[22] Much drama with an identifiable religious element turns out to be 'secular', in R. M. Frye's sense:[23] that element belongs to the second category.

In order to demonstrate Webster's Calvinism, one has to identify the Calvinist doctrines his plays project, and argue that the final position confirms the soundness of the doctrine. Let us consider some of the difficulties the demonstration involves. The sense of humanity as 'incurably corrupt' is common to many doctrines within the Christian religion; it is in their solutions to this situation that they differ. Calvin's solution is distinguished by its logic and consistency. He asserts that all men are sinful. There is a double predestination, however, for the elect and the reprobate; grace is imputed to the one, and refused to the other. The elect must walk in good works, and seek constantly for assurance from God that though sinful they will yet be saved. The reprobate, easily identified by their conduct, cannot be saved and should be cast forth from the godly community. The evil-doers are certainly reprobate; those who manifest good works are not necessarily of the elect, though the elect will certainly exhibit these signs.

[22] This view of *The Merchant of Venice* is argued by Nevill Coghill, in 'The Governing Idea: Essays in the Interpretation of Shakespeare', *Shakespeare Quarterly*, i (1948).

[23] R. M. Frye, *Shakespeare and Christian Doctrine*, (Princeton University Press, Princeton, N.J., 1963), p. 7.

The followers and successors of Calvin did not view the matter with the same iron logic. For him, election was without merit; conviction of it no proof; good works no guarantee. In later practice, it worked differently. 'The true Calvinist came to think that assurance of salvation was possible on earth, that the saints knew they were saved and had God on their side, and that success implied divine approval and favour.'[24] The characteristic inquiry of later Calvinism is into the relationship between salvation and works. The records of Calvinist psychology, in England and New England as elsewhere, constantly reveal the agonized self-probings of the individual mind for signs of grace, for assurance that salvation would be granted. Equally, they often reveal a self-satisfied conviction of grace as following automatically from their knowledge of walking in good works. Still, the Calvinist mind is directed towards the problems of election. And this is not the same thing as ceasing to do evil.

It is easily shown, then, that the doctrines of Calvin and the practice of his followers, taken together, contain central anomalies and inconsistencies. It would thus be difficult at any time to assign a precise place to Webster within the Calvinist movement. But if we assume that Webster's tragedies reflect his religious beliefs in any way, and if we assume moreover that a Calvinist is capable of writing a play at all—two very large assumptions—we can profitably ask: what is there, in *The White Devil*, that is at least reminiscent of Calvinism?

There is certainly a clear division of dramatis personae, the evil-doers and the good. But this is not the same as the damned and the elect. If it were so, Calvinism would be a much simpler phenomenon than it is. Webster displays no interest at all in the psychological problems attached to election—which are, perhaps, the most inviting area of Calvinism to a dramatist of parts. Instead, repentance is presented as a simple dramatic possibility. Antonelli and Gasparo urge it upon Lodovico:

> The law doth somtimes mediate, thinkes it good
> Not ever to steepe violent sinnes in blood,
> This gentle pennance may both end your crimes,
> And in the example better these bad times.
>
> (I. i. 34–7)

---

[24] G. R. Elton, *Reformation Europe 1517–1559* (Collins, London, 1963), p. 219.

The purely social, empirical force of these lines is given theological status by the later words of the Pope, who again warns
Lodovico of the dangers he incurs:

> Miserable creature!
> If thou persist in this, 't is damnable.
> And so I leave thee
> With all the Furies hanging bout thy necke,
> Till by thy penitence thou remove this evill,
> In conjuring from thy breast that cruell Devill.
>   (iv. iii. 119–20, 127–30)

Repentance, and thus the avoidance of damnation, is twice presented as a feasible path. Vittoria gets a similar chance, at the
House of Convertites. She, Brachiano, and Flamineo all have to
endure lay sermons by Cornelia, Marcello, and Isabella that
assume the possibility of repentance. Of course one can argue
that Lodovico and the others do not repent because they cannot,
and are thus damned anyway. The fact is that *The White Devil*
presents to the audience repentance as a perfectly possible, if unlikely, course of conduct. Without the possibility, and the refusal
to take the opportunity, the dramatic tensions in the play are
somewhat reduced.

Still, the major characters of *The White Devil* appear strongly,
indeed inexorably, impelled along the path they follow. Mr.
Baker-Smith has stressed this aspect of the matter, in his long
and subtle account of Webster's religion. 'We may take it that
he did not write with the *Institutes* open before him but determinism is in the air.'[25] I should however be slightly more cautious
in welcoming the implications of determinism to Webster's work.
What, I think, emerges from all these of his plays is a distinction
between external circumstance, which may be ineluctable, and
the inner freedom to define oneself in act against external
circumstance. Thus, when Flamineo says (in a passage which
Mr. Baker-Smith cites as in keeping with the general determinism of the play) 'Fate's a Spaniell,/We cannot beat it from us',
this admission does not determine Flamineo's reaction. And it is
the nature of the reaction, surely, that fascinates Webster, not
the consideration that all reactions are equally irrelevant.

What, then, are we left with in *The White Devil*? I think that

[25] Dominic Baker-Smith, 'Religion and John Webster', in *John Webster*, ed.
Brian Morris (Ernest Benn, London, 1970), p. 216.

Mr. Baker-Smith's reading of the situation is the right one. Discussing the Calvinist background to Webster, he writes:

This is not to claim any clear theological commitment in Webster's work but a playwright has a particular end in view, to arouse the feelings of the audience and to order these feelings according to a pattern. To work on an audience in this way it is essential that the playwright touch on sensitive areas; he must know the raw nerves of his audience, if only by instinct.[26]

Again, of Brachiano's deathbed ravings: 'The tirades are really directed at the religious consciousness of the audience in order to elicit from darker pockets of the imagination the horror that the resources of the theatre could not hope to convey.'[27] It follows naturally from the account of Webster that I give in Part One of this study, that I am ready to see Webster's religious allusions as an extension of his sensationalism. The horror of the hereafter complements the physical horror of the stage. Such a reading is confirmed, for me, by the consideration that Webster's philosophical and psychological concerns seem largely unrelated to the central Calvinist issues.[28] This will become much more apparent in the discussion of what I regard as Webster's existentialism (see pages 126–49), which can be seen to some extent in *The White Devil* but much more in *The Duchess of Malfi*. That play, as I argue later, depicts a universe without God in which man is free to generate his own values and to act on them. Such a philosophy simply fails to relate at all to the Calvinist framework. So the status of evil in *The White Devil* remains on the level of metaphor. The metaphors are varied, powerful, suggestive. But they lack, and are meant to lack, theological precision and commitment.

2. THE LAW

The Law stands, in *The White Devil*, in massive confrontation with evil. The law theme manifests itself in a variety of terms: law, reward, salary, service, payment, justice, revenge, storm, punishment, fate. These counters bear several implications, and

[26] Ibid., p. 210.

[27] Ibid., p. 221.

[28] It should be pointed out that Lucas, in his notes on 'the Helvetian translation' (*The Duchess of Malfi*, IV. ii. 95), regards the passage as a satire on the Calvinists. Lucas, ii. 183.

must not be subject to too limited an interpretation. Travis Bogard, who rightly emphasizes the importance of the opening scene and its discussion of reward and punishment, analyses the play in terms of 'courtly reward and punishment'. He recognizes three elements: the rottenness of court life, the evils of social parasitism, and the capriciousness of a prince's reward. And on Lodovico's final speech, he comments: 'The spectacle of courtly reward and punishment has run its course; the horrors are summed up; the courtly way of life is seen without illusion.'[29] This theme, then, culminates in Vittoria's dying couplet:

> O happy they that never saw the Court,
> "Nor ever knew great Man but by report.
>
> (v. vi. 261–2)

All this is perfectly true, and represents part of Webster's fable. Yet to see the theme simply as an indictment of the ills of the Jacobean/Italian courts presents Webster as a social satirist, but ignores his inquiry into the nature of the tragedy. The intellectual weight of the play's third line falls on *reward*, rather than 'courtly'. It is this theme of reward and punishment that embodies the tragic issues.

'Banisht!' cries Lodovico: and this motto-theme is at once laid before the audience. The situation is punishment rejected; and it complements the situation at the end of the play, which is punishment accepted: the rack, the gallows, and the torturing-wheel. The opening and close of *The White Devil* plainly compose an ordered design. This design can best be studied through four characters: Lodovico, Brachiano, Vittoria, and Flamineo.

Lodovico's posture is a rebellion against law.

> Ha, ha, ô *Democritus* thy Gods
> That governe the whole world! Courtly reward
> And punishment. Fortune's a right whore.
> If she give ought, she deales it in smal percels,
> That she may take away all at one swope.
>
> (I. i. 2–6)

The cold, judicial voice of Antonelli makes itself heard. 'Come my Lord,/You are justly dom'd' (I. i. 12–13). Antonelli enumerates his reasons. We are left in no doubt of the matter. The punishment is just; the responsibility is Lodovico's. He cannot

---

[29] Bogard, op. cit., pp. 127–8.

see it. Reward and punishment are for him merely a matter of
luck, a jade's trick of that whore Fortune. He has 'great enemies'
—that is his trouble. Lodovico's is the perennial attitude of the
malcontent who will blame anyone, anything for his situation but
himself. He will have none of Gasparo's

> The law doth somtimes mediate, thinkes it good
> Not ever to steepe violent sinnes in blood.
> This gentle pennance may both end your crimes,
> And in the example better these bad times.
>
> (I. i. 34–7)

It is a warning which Lodovico does not heed, nor that of
Monticelso. But at the play's end, Lodovico not only accepts but
claims that individual responsibility for his acts which he had
denied in the beginning:

> I do glory yet,
> That I can call this act mine owne:
>
> (v. vi. 295–6)

This surge of exultance yields to the final note of acceptance:

> For my part,
> The racke, the gallowes, and the torturing wheele
> Shall bee but sound sleepes to me, here's my rest—
> "I limb'd this night-peece and it was my best.
>
> (v. vi. 296–9)

The wheel has come full circle. The punishment is accepted; the
reward is just.

Paulo Ursini, Duke of Brachiano, also learns something in the
course of the action of the nature of law and punishment. The
infatuate nobleman, sighing his praises over Vittoria, murmurs
to her:

> I'le seate you above the law and above scandall.
>
> (I. ii. 253)

'Above scandall': Vittoria is soon to be dragged through a public
court, sentenced to live among prostitutes, fated to hear Brachiano say:

> For all the world speakes ill of thee.
>
> (IV. ii. 103)

'Above the law': Vittoria may evade human law, but not that of
the Fates.

The irony, keen enough here, is scarifying when Brachiano, engaging a poisoner to dispose of his wife, assures him:'

> Noble friend
> You bind me ever to you—this shall stand
> As the firm seale annexed to my hand.
> It shall inforce a payment.
> (II. ii. 51–4)

'It shall enforce a payment': the line finds its counterpart in the scene when Brachiano is writhing under the poisoner's hands. Crime and punishment are exactly poised; and the mad Brachiano mutters, 'Indeed I am to blame . . .' (v. iii. 87). He, too, accepts justice at the last.

The ravings of the madman should not be dismissed. As is now generally agreed, the mad scene in *The Duchess of Malfi* (IV. ii) has a structural importance; Webster has fully assimilated the idea of 'reason in madness' (*King Lear*, IV. vi. 173). Lodovico makes the same point, with

> His minde fastens
> On twentie severall objects, which confound
> Deepe Sence with follie.
> (v. iii. 72–4)

There is indeed a 'Deepe Sence' in Brachiano's admitting that he is to blame. There is likewise a significance in

> Make up your accountes;
> Ile now bee mine owne Steward.
> (v. iii. 85–6)

The legal-accounting imagery extends the theme of law and retribution; and 'Ile now bee mine owne Steward' repeats the idea of personal responsibility. (The phrase is an important one for Webster—he uses it in Flamineo's 'Ide rather . . . be mine owne ostler' (III. iii. 3–5) and Bosola's 'I'll be mine own eexample' (v. iv. 95).) The last phase of Brachiano's life has a dramatic appropriateness that should not be obscured by his madness.

Vittoria, like Lodovico, rejects the charges made against her. Although her defence in court is a high dramatic point, the real charge is moral rather than legal; and it is made earlier, by Cornelia: 'Woe to light hearts!—they still forerun our fall!' (I.

ii. 259) Vittoria palters, ascribing her compromising situation to passion:

> I do protest if any chast deniall,
> If any thing but bloud could have alayed
> His long suit to me . . .
>
> (I. ii. 283–5)

This is a strange, and unconvincing denial of personal responsibility. Her liaison leads her to the court; we need not linger over that, save to point out that for Vittoria the scene constitutes a further and massive denial of responsibility. That is a public affair; the inwardness of the matter is exposed when she upbraids Brachiano for her punishment:

> Is this your palace? . . .
> Is't not your high preferment?
>
> (IV. ii. 115, 119)

A little later comes

> and I do wish
> That I could make you full Executor
> To all my sinnes—
>
> (IV. ii. 125–7)

The legal terminology, as in some of the preceding quotations, accords well with the larger concept of the Law that Webster has in mind. Once again we see that fatal desire to renounce responsibility for one's acts. Vittoria and Brachiano exactly parallel each other here; the essential situation of the quarrel scene is that each is blaming the other, instead of himself. The core of the scene is:

> *Vittoria.*   You did name your Dutchesse.
> *Brachiano.*   Whose death God pardon.
> *Vittoria.*   Whose death God revenge
>   On thee most godlesse Duke.
>
> (IV. ii. 105–8)

There is grave, judicial irony here. All this recrimination is to no purpose. No one can be the 'Executor' of one's sins except oneself. Vittoria will grumble yet that

> Your dog or hawke should be rewarded better
> Then I have bin.
>
> (IV. ii. 193–4)

But at the last she too is to realize that the responsibility lies nearer home. 'O my greatest sinne lay in my blood' (v. vi. 240). And her final breath is of payment: 'Now my blood paies for't' (v. vi. 241). Again comes the note of acceptance, the recognition that justice has been done. Vittoria's last words echo the 'blood' idea quoted above, but now with a punning acceptance of the fitness of 'blood' paying.

There remains Flamineo. With him the whole idea is seen at its most explicit. He is concerned, quite simply, with making his way in the world. He is prepared to commit crime to further his career; and the word 'payment' is never far from his lips. His materialist philosophy is outlined in the first act (I. ii. 301-48). He is sceptical, talking with Marcello, about the rewards of virtue:

> what hast got
> But like the wealth of Captaines, a poore handfull?—
> Which in they palme thou bear'st, as men hold water—
> Seeking to gripe it fast, the fraile reward
> Steales through thy fingers.
>
> (III. i. 41-5)

Flamineo's reaction to his sister's disgrace is: 'Is this the end of service?' (III. iii. 3) Agonizedly he addresses the English Ambassador:

> Here they sell justice with those weights
> they press men to death with. O horrible
> salarie!
> (III. iii. 26-8)

The 'horrible salarie', as Flamineo seems to apprehend, is soon to be his. The final scene demonstrates the matter clearly. Flamineo approaches Vittoria with:

> *Flamineo.*   You are my Lords Executrix, and I claime
>   Reward, for my long service.
> *Vittoria.*   For your service?
>   (v. vi. 8-9)

Vittoria had wished that Brachiano could be the 'Executor' for her sins (IV. ii. 125-7). Now she is the 'Executrix'; she cannot dispose of her sins thus easily; indeed she must bear Brachiano's. The icy justice of Vittoria's reply to Flamineo parallels Antonelli's 'You are justly dom'd':

Vittoria.   I will read it.
I give that portion to thee, and no other
Which *Caine* gron'd under having slaine his brother.
(v. vi. 13–15)

The implications of this judgement remain to be elaborated. Flamineo, in a flash of self-realization, says

My life hath done service to other men,
My death shall serve mine own turne.
(v. vi. 50–1)

Service finds its payment, and Flamineo admits with it

Fate's a Spaniell,
Wee cannot beat it from us.
(v. vi. 178–9)

All that remains is the responsibility of the individual:

I doe not looke
Who went before, nor who shall follow mee;
Noe, at my selfe I will begin and end.
(v. vi. 256–8)

The parallels between the spiritual progresses of these four characters are thus seen to be close, and striking. Each of them commits acts of sin; each rebels, with every particle of his vitality, against the punishment; each accepts, at the last, the justice of the reward.

Lodovico.   I do glory yet,
That I can call this act mine owne: For my part,
The racke, the gallowes, and the torturing wheele
Shall bee but sound sleepes to me, here's my rest—
"I limb'd this night-peece and it was my best.
(v. vi. 295–9)

Brachiano.   Indeed I am to blame . . .
(v. iii. 87)

Vittoria.   O my greatest sinne lay in my blood.
Now my blood paies for't.
(v. vi. 240–1)

Flamineo.   Fate's a Spaniell,
               Wee cannot beat it from us.

                            (v. vi. 178–9)

So much is clear. We have now, however, to clarify the concepts underlying these quotations. It is not necessary to explore the semantic distinctions in the terms Webster uses—law, service, payment, reward, justice, fate, punishment. They merge imperceptibly with one another. I discern two main ideas emerging from these repeated terms, in which the beginning and end of a character's stage progress are so carefully matched. First, they imply a statement of the human mechanisms of action and reaction. Sin will bring on its retribution unfailingly—an impression strengthened by the play's many images of storm, itself a symbol of retribution. Second, human beings are responsible for their actions. This is the only conclusion that can be drawn from the acceptance of personal responsibility that each of the four characters demonstrates at the point of death.

In sum, these terms, embodying the ideas of personal responsibility and the inevitability of retribution, amount to a statement concerning the mechanisms of justice. The language of the play is intimately related to its plot, an ironic process of retribution. Irony is the Law in action. And this form of justice—we need not call it the 'Divine Law'—is to be distinguished from human justice, the justice of the courts. The great Trial scene, the play's dramatic ritual of justice, shows the social law to be fallible and corrupt; neither prosecution nor defence inspires confidence. Therefore, the legal and quasi-legal terminology adopted by the dramatis personae conceals another irony, the implicit contrast between human justice and the true mechanisms of retribution. And this irony extends to the final curtain. The closing lines are given to Giovanni, who metes out justice; a further proof of Webster's serious concern with the concept. But if we believe the social justice that Giovanni represents to be absolute, we shall have to face Gunnar Boklund's shrewd question: are we not entitled to remember Flamineo's previous reference to Giovanni, 'He hath his Unckles villanous looke already,/In decimo sexto' (v. iv. 25–6)?[30] How can we be sure that the old cycle is not beginning again, that here is not another Brachiano in the

---

[30] Gunnar Boklund, *The Sources of The White Devil* (Uppsala, 1957), p. 179.

making—or Francisco, or Monticelso? Is not the quality of justice eroded by the quality of the justicers? J. R. Brown well says: 'There is no answer; the play leaves us with a sense of insecurity.'[31]

3. CONCLUSION

The themes of evil and the Law meet in the final scenes, and combine in an impression that is artistically and theatrically satisfying. The play's design of imagery, character, and action has a logical resolution. Evil has been constantly invoked in the imagery; manifest in the actions of the characters; satisfyingly punished, with the maximum of ironic appropriateness; and justice suitably acknowledged in the final words of the sinners. Irony pervades the whole, but justice—of a sort—is done, and seen to be done.

But tragedy is not simply about justice, though it is deeply concerned with it. Even in *The White Devil*, the deaths of Marcello, Isabella, and Cornelia have nothing to do with justice, though they make small demands on our attention and are quite outside the play's focus. The highest form of tragedy, by general consent, explores the frontiers of justice and injustice, the extent to which humanity co-operates with its fate to bring about its own downfall. The task which Webster set himself in his next major essay in tragedy was twofold. The centre of his tragedy was to be a heroine whose fate was not a simple matter of sin and punishment; and his agent of tragedy was to develop the idea of personal responsibility stated, but not elaborated, in *The White Devil*. The themes of evil and the Law are continued, but with subtly changed emphasis, in *The Duchess of Malfi*.

[31] Brown, *The White Devil*, p. lviii.

III

THE DUCHESS OF MALFI

The Duchess of Malfi traverses much of the same ground as *The White Devil*; yet it is a critical error to view it simply as a better-organized repeat performance. What changes *The Duchess of Malfi* radically is the emergence of a virtually new theme, that of knowledge. The intellectual drama of *The Duchess of Malfi* lies in the interaction of the ideas of human evil, the limits of human knowledge, and the Law. I shall concentrate on the knowledge theme because it is this, changing the relations of the other two themes to each other and to the whole work, that makes *The Duchess of Malfi* essentially a new play and not a revision.

1. EVIL

The leading characters in *The White Devil* are all malefactors, and their fate exhibits a simple pattern of crime and punishment. In *The Duchess of Malfi*, the searchlight of interest shifts towards the pole of good; it picks out Antonio and his Duchess, who though far from blameless are brought to a tragedy of suffering. They, the victims, confront the play's predators, Ferdinand and the Cardinal; in the middle stands Bosola, a grey zone of warring good and ill. The effect is subtler, better balanced. Yet para-doxically, it is a far more pessimistic play. Its predecessor, while stressing the mechanisms of retribution, held out a formal hope of repentance, avoidance of sin, justice. *The Duchess of Malfi* does not postulate an ordered universe at all. It offers a vision of a meaningless universe, a context for humanity irretrievably prone to corruption and error, a situation in which the individual has no recourse but to generate his own values and to decide on his own course of action, futile though it may be.

(a) Evil Explicit: Witches and Devils
A sense of evil, as before, hangs miasmatically around the char-acters. It seems, almost, as tangible as mist rising above the

ruined walls of the past, those visual symbols of mortality. It is
codified most explicitly in the references to 'devils' and to
Machiavellianism: 'polliticke', 'great men', 'princes', together
with 'court', which serves as a general symbol of social corruption. They naturally underscore as evil the actions of Ferdinand
and the Cardinal, and Bosola's service to them. What is interesting is the insistent suggestion they provide that the Duchess and
Antonio are a part of the play's corruption. 'Witch', for example,
a term related to 'devil', is repeatedly applied to the Duchess.

> *Ferdinand.*   For they whose faces do belye their hearts,
> Are Witches, ere they arrive at twenty yeeres,
> I: and give the divell sucke.
>
> (I. i. 343–5)

The appearance-reality opposition, always with Webster the
model of evil, strengthens the counters of 'witch' and 'devil'.
Ferdinand is naturally no spokesman for a just view of the
Duchess, yet he is right in anticipating the clandestine nature of
her conduct. And the 'witch' point is repeated (III. i. 94; III. ii.
164–5). Witchcraft here, as J. R. Brown observes, 'has become
a synonym for the power of sex'.[32] These are hints of an affinity
between Vittoria and the Duchess—stronger than the Victorian
critics would have admitted. The 'rancke blood' (III. i. 94) recalls
Vittoria's 'O my greatest sinne lay in my blood.' The technical
difference—and it is an advance—is that Vittoria's statement is a
personal admission of virtually absolute status, while Ferdinand's
testimony is that of an unstable witness, which we are at liberty
to accept partially or to reject. The evidence of the disturbed or
mad is not, in a Websterian play, to be rejected on that account
alone.

One need not rely on that testimony. Even the wooing scene
contains a strong hint of the latent evil. Antonio, dazzled by the
prospect, breathes

> There is a sawcy, and ambitious divell
> Is dauncing in this circle.
>
> (I. i. 471–2)

The Duchess takes up the metaphor:

> There needs small conjuration, when your finger
> May doe it.   (I. i. 475–6)

[32] Brown, *The Duchess of Malfi*, p. xliv.

I do not think this exchange can be construed as indicating that Webster views the liaison as necessarily immoral. It does, however, suggest that the liaison is the product of the devil Ambition's tempting. No doubt there are degrees of devils—Flamineo says as much—but devil the tempter remains.

And hell is constantly invoked. In *The Duchess of Malfi* it seems primarily to symbolize the state of mind of the principals, rather than to identify a theological concept. But all of them speak of it. The Duchess sees life as 'the greatest torture soules feele in hell,/In hell' (IV. i. 82–3). In as great mental extremity, Ferdinand cries

> had I bin damn'd in hell,
> And should have heard of this, it would have put me
> Into a cold sweat.
>
> (II. v. 97–9)

For the disillusioned Bosola, life is 'this sencible Hell' (IV. ii. 369); the only question that disturbs the Cardinal is the nature of hell-fire (v. v. 1–7). The extreme mental anguish, as much as the moral evil of the characters, finds as its symbol hell.

Such terms compose a running commentary on the psychological and moral situation of the principals. The emphasis is quite clear, and I stress the number of 'devil' references in the exposition, most noticeably in the Ferdinand-Bosola transaction. 'Devil' has however a certain ambivalence. The word embraces two areas of thought, folk-lore and religion. As I have suggested, the term is not sufficiently well defined to justify its place in any formal theological scheme. The devil references here link with the idea of witchcraft, and seem to belong to the world of superstition and country proverbs.[33]

(b) *The Model of Evil: Appearance and Reality*

The idea of appearance-reality is as important here as in *The White Devil*. The plot is a series of variations on the concept. All are deceived: the lovers in their apparent security, Bosola in the reward for his service, Ferdinand in the fulfilment of his revenge, and the Cardinal in the exercise of his Machiavellian arts. Many of these ironies have been analysed by Hereward T. Price in his

[33] Morris P. Tilley lists over 170 proverbs that refer to the Devil. Morris P. Tilley, *A Dictionary of the Proverbs in England in the Sixteenth and Seventeenth Centuries* (University of Michigan Press, Ann Arbor, Mich., 1950).

paper on Webster's imagery.[34] I cite here the appearance-reality images because they express, besides the quality of irony, clear indications of Webster's concept of evil and its relevance to the actions of his characters.

The point about these images is that they fix the idea of *deception as evil* very firmly upon the Duchess, and Bosola. This is important, because it is not immediately obvious—and it is far from being a critical truism—that Bosola does wrong in becoming an intelligencer (as distinct from assassin), and that the Duchess errs in arranging a secret marriage for herself. Yet this conclusion is marked. The devil references in the first act, for example, which cluster round the Ferdinand-Bosola bargain, present the devil as a creature of fair seeming: 'Sometimes the Divell doth preach' (I. i. 317), and 'Thus the Divell/Candies all sinnes o'er '(I. i. 299–300). This concept of the devil is old: 'the devil hath power/To assume a pleasing shape.' It is a suggestive commentary on the several disguises worn by Bosola. As with Vittoria, and the Duchess, our sympathies may be involved, but the imagery damns them.

Generally, the antithesis is of fair seeming and corrupt interior, not the converse. But the core passages are surely those which fasten the idea upon mortality itself, not merely upon the schemers and Machiavellians. Bosola speaks of 'shadowes/Of wealth and painted honors . . .' (III. ii. 320–1), a phrase repeated in 'Off my painted honour!' (IV. ii. 362) The Duchess, for Cariola, is 'Like to your picture in the gallery, /A deale of life in shew, but none in practise' (IV. ii. 33–4). And there is a repetition of a crucial *sententia* from *The White Devil*:

> *Bosola.* "Glories (like glowe-wormes) afarre off, shine bright,
> But look'd to neere, have neither heate, nor light.
>   (IV. ii. 141–2)

These images invoke the sense of hollowness and transitoriness of all earthly things; but especially the glitter of the Court. They integrate with all images of bodily corruption and death. The 'painting' images link with Bosola's outburst against the Old Lady's cosmetics (II. i)—a fragment of satire that merges easily with the ensuing meditation.

The counter-image follows logically:

[34] Hereward T. Price, op. cit.

Duchess.   so we
          Are forc'd to expresse our violent passions
          In ridles, and in dreames, and leave the path
          Of simple vertue, which was never made
          To seeme the thing it is not.
                              (I. i. 510–14)

This statement bears the whole weight of the anti-Machiavellian
ideal in this play. It stands most obviously in opposition to her
brothers' tactics:

Ferdinand.   So—I will onely study to seeme
               The thing I am not:
                              (II. v. 81–2)

Cardinal.   I would not be seene in't.
                              (I. i. 236)

There are two important implications in these passages. They
point unmistakably towards a concept of the body as being inherently evil; because the fair surface is necessarily a façade to the
inner corruption of mortality, and thus a further variant of the
model of evil. And they suggest that the Duchess's action in
marrying Antonio was sinful because it involved scheming and
deception, leaving 'the path of simple vertue'. Naturally, the
other main considerations that apply to the Duchess's marriage
remain valid. The theological arguments concerning the supposed
immorality of a widow's remarriage retain their relevance; the
social justification that the Duchess had no choice, given the
attitude of her brothers, is legitimate. Webster surely means to
present a complex and debatable event. But the imagery implies
a consistent judgement. Whatever her motives, whatever her
justifications, the outcome of the Duchess's action is undeniable.
Her sin lies in choosing a course in which reality is, of necessity,
divorced from appearance.

(c) *Evil in Metaphor: Animalism*
As in *The White Devil*, the animal images continuously underscore the action. The range is even greater; well over sixty
different *sorts* of animal are alluded to in *The Duchess of Malfi*.
Only one, however, stands out: the wolf. And as before, the
effect is to advance the notion of the brute in man, an aspect of
evil.

The links between man and beast are quite explicit; it is not a matter that needs to be inferred from the sheer quantity of animal imagery. Ferdinand's lycanthropy dramatizes the beast in man, and this turn of the plot is the working-out of the theme stated earlier by Bosola. His 'meditation', in which Webster holds up the action to state with the utmost emphasis a matter of fundamental import, opens thus:

> What thing is in this outward forme of man
> To be belov'd? we account it ominous,
> If Nature doe produce a Colt, or Lambe,
> A Fawne, or Goate, in any limbe resembling
> A Man; and flye from't as a prodegy.
> Man stands amaz'd to see his deformity,
> In any other Creature but himselfe.
> But in our owne flesh, though we beare diseases
> Which have their true names onely tane from beasts,
> As the most ulcerous Woolfe, and swinish Meazeall;
> Though we are eaten up of lice, and wormes,
> And though continually we beare about us
> A rotten and dead body, we delight
> To hide it in rich tissew—all our feare,
> (Nay all our terrour) is, least our Phisition
> Should put us in the ground, to be made sweete.
>
> (II. i. 47–62)

This is a formal statement of affinities. The body images reinforce the animal, and the animal images reinforce the body. And 'rich tissew' again crystallizes the appearance-reality motif.

The animal images bear upon all, directly or indirectly; but most of them stem from Bosola and Ferdinand. Bosola is the play's focus, at once the manipulator of the action, the main internal view, and the embodiment of the tragic issues. A point made through him carries greater weight than from anyone else. Quite simply, he sees life in animal terms. It is not a pathological trait; his language has none of the demented overtones of Ferdinand's. Bosola's is a much more neutral view, the approach to life of the cynic, not the psychopath. Typically:

He, and his brother, are like Plum-trees (that grow crooked over standing-pooles) they are rich, and ore-laden with Fruite, but none but Crowes, Pyes, and Catter-pillers feed on them: Could I be one of their

flattring Panders, I would hang on their eares like a horse-leach, till I
were full, and then drop off.

(I. i. 50–5)

doe these Lyce drop off now?

(III. ii. 275)

His language to the Old Lady, on the subject of her closet, is in
the fullest sense bestial. (II. i. 37–41) Here it might be argued
that the Old Lady is, by Bosola's standards, a fit subject for
indecency. But even the Duchess evokes associations which indicate his cast of mind. From his statement that his corruption
'grew out of horse-doong' (I. i. 312–13) stems naturally the
apricot dialogue of II. i., leading to the discovery of the Duchess's
condition. It is as though Bosola's singularly bestial cast of mind
had embraced the Duchess. He can refer to her 'most vulterous
eating' (II. ii. 2) and hint at her sexual proclivities in the
'English mastiffe' comparison (IV. i. 15). Bosola is the lens
through which we see much of the action; and across that lens
stalk perpetually visions of beasts that superimpose themselves
upon the men and women of the stage.

Ferdinand is a study of the beast in man. With Bosola, the
animal images represent only a part of his character; the conflict
is there, but the animal references die away in the closing scenes
as Bosola's 'good nature' asserts itself. With Ferdinand, the
opposite progression occurs. Animal images are always present
in his thoughts, even in the early scenes; towards the end they
thicken noticeably, paralleling his lapse into pure animality. The
break in control comes with the news of the Duchess's liaison,
immediately visualized in animal terms:

Me thinkes I see her laughing,
Excellent *Hyenna*—

(II. v. 52–3)

The image blends with the obscene visions of copulation that
chase across his mind. Thereafter his talk becomes increasingly
animal-obsessed: 'Basilisque', 'wolfe', 'screech-Owle', 'dogs',
'monkeys', 'Paraqueto' reveal the drift. By the time of his final
interview with his sister, her children are 'Cubbs'. And she dies
with words that pick out with appalling clarity the brutish nature
of Ferdinand and his brother:

> Go tell my brothers, when I am laid out,
> They then may feede in quiet.
>
> (IV. ii. 243–4)

Thereafter the wolf, 'that's foe to men', takes over his faculties. The last act contains the consummation of his incarnate animalism.

Ferdinand's is the extreme instance of imagery which is organic, as opposed to decorative. The links between the characters and the animals are, at any time, obvious enough. But with Ferdinand image, character, and plot attain a complete fusion. It is the *ne plus ultra* of Webster's achievement in this sphere.

(d) Evil in Metaphor: The Body and Corruption

I find some fifty images of sickness, corruption, and physic in *The Duchess of Malfi*. And they are extended by a large mass of imagery about which one cannot be precise at all, that is, images of the body. This is not a matter for exact definition, since no clear border line can be drawn between bodily functions and other areas of human thought and activity. But a large number of images asserts the presence of the body—in its totality, its parts, its actions, its sensations, its sickness. The physical apprehension of the body weighs heavily upon *The Duchess of Malfi*.

The matter is given explicit and repeated emphasis. The formal subject of Bosola's disquisition is the body:

> What thing is in this outward forme of man
> To be belov'd?

And after drawing on the various animal affinities, he concludes:

> And though continually we beare about us
> A rotten and dead body, we delight
> To hide it in rich tissew—all our feare,
> (Nay all our terrour) is, least our Phisition
> Should put us in the ground, to be made sweete.
>
> (II. i. 58–62)

The body symbolizes not life and beauty, but mortality. This concept receives formal reiteration on two occasions in the fourth act, when Bosola as tombmaker and bellman delivers what are virtually lay sermons. To the Duchess's question, 'Who am I?' he dilates on the relationship of body and soul:

Thou art a box of worme-seede, at best, but a salvatory of greene mummey: what's this flesh? a little cruded milke, phantasticall puffe-paste: our bodies are weaker then those paper prisons boyes use to keepe flies in: more contemptible: since ours is to preserve earth-wormes: didst thou ever see a Larke in a cage? such is the soule in the body: this world is like her little turfe of grasse, and the Heaven ore our heades, like her looking glasse, onely gives us a miserable know-ledge of the small compasse of our prison.

(IV. ii. 122–31)

The speaker and the dramatic context give these images extra-ordinary potency, and revive the old *de contemptu mundi* theme. And Bosola's dirge for the Duchess points to the ultimate destina-tion of the body:

> Much you had of land and rent,
> Your length in clay's now competent.

(IV. ii. 184–5)

In addition to this formal emphasis, the body receives compelling theatrical images. The parallels which Bosola draws between the body and a prison provide a symbolic commentary on the literal fact of the Duchess's imprisonment. And the echo scene presents the body, compared with a ruined building; a parallel which Antonio draws:

> Churches, and Citties (which have diseases like to men)
> Must have like death that we have.

(v. iii. 19–20)

and Bosola completes:

> We are onely like dead wals, or vaulted graves,
> That ruin'd, yeildes no eccho:

(v. v. 121–2)

All this is verbally explicit, and connected with visual sym-bols. Moreover, much of the play's verbal imagery suggests more subtly the existence of the body. Of the body's parts, the eye, ear, and heart are often named. All fit into the general body pattern; they stand for imperfection. The body itself is 'rotten', and 'dead'. The heart is 'rotten', 'dead', 'bleeding', 'left-hand side'; the eye is 'sore', 'dazzled', or 'blind'; the ear is 'deaf'. Always there is the implication that the body is not vital, but mortal.

The body in action is also presented in highly controlled imagery. One notes especially the images of feeding, an activity associated with Ferdinand and the Cardinal; they suggest a peculiarly gross form of relationship.[35] More generally, the verbs of action convey the quality of strain and violence. There is little feeling of normality, of relaxed and customary action. Thus, Antonio's land is 'ravish'd from his throate/By the Cardinals entreaty' (v. i. 48–9). The Duchess will 'plant my soule in mine eares, to heare you' (III. ii. 89). She dies imploring the executioners to 'pull downe heaven' upon her (IV. ii. 237–8). 'Will you racke me?' asks the Cardinal of his mistress (v. ii. 265). Even in his calmer moments, Ferdinand has

> Let me have his beard saw'd off, and his eye-browes
> Fil'd more civill.
>
> (v. ii. 56–7)

These eccentric, strained verbs typify the images of action. The words are, in their context, as forced as the violence they imply. The violence of the action finds often this queer similitude in the images of the body in action.

The body's sensations have already been discussed (pages 22–4); they consistently figure pain and feverishness. These, of course, find their dramatic expression in the fourth act, the prolonged torture of the Duchess. Such images accompany those of sickness, corruption, and physic. There is no lack of illustration. The ills of the body range over galls, palsy, madness, tetter, leprosy, imposthume, toothache, apoplexy, catarrh, cough, consumption, plague, and ague. The most important is the ague; it is named in three critical passages, and like the plague is linked with images of sensation. It becomes a striking symbol for the human condition in Antonio's 'Pleasure of life, what is't? onely the good houres/Of an Ague' (v. iv. 78–9). The ague apart, there is nothing to compare with the syphilis images of *The White Devil*. Syphilis itself is given little prominence in the later play. So far as I can observe, it is mentioned only by Bosola (II. i. 42–3) as an immediate prefix to his meditation on the body: 'I do wonder you doe not loath your selves—observe my meditation now . . .' Syphilis represents not a bawdy joke, nor yet the idea of retribution, but the inner rottenness of the body.

---

[35] I. i. 54; I. i. 183; IV. i. 168; IV. ii. 204; IV. ii. 244.

The images of corruption and poison reinforce this idea. They all stem from Antonio's initial statement of the motto-theme:

> A Princes Court
> Is like a common Fountaine, whence should flow
> Pure silver-droppes in generall: But if't chance
> Some curs'd example poyson't neere the head,
> "Death, and diseases through the whole land spread.
>
> (I. i. 12–16)

Now this, following as it does the description of good government, sets the pattern of the play. The Arragonian brothers poison the fountain of their realm at the head, and from their evil flows their subjects' evil. (This consequence is most literally expressed in the poisoning of Julia.) Moreover, the following lines state the remedy, and foreshadow Bosola's role. The responsibility rests with a prince's servants to advise him well (I. i. 17–23), a duty Bosola notably fails to execute. The timing is ironically precise here. Even as Antonio finishes saying, 'It is a noble duety to informe them/What they ought to fore-see', he switches to 'Here comes Bosola. . . .'

That is the argument: bad government corrupts a realm. It does so via the plague-bearer Bosola, himself corrupted by the Prince. Bosola's corruption grows, as he says, out of horse-dung; an important image that combines the ideas of Ferdinand's responsibility for the appointment, Bosola's rottenness, and the trick he is to serve the Duchess. His 'corruption' however merges with a larger rottenness, with the 'rotten and dead body' of the meditation. Here the corruption is inescapable, and mortal. It is a wider perspective.

For this corrupt state of humanity, physic is useless. The idea is introduced with an immediate ironic turn. The Duchess, on the point of proposing, says

> One of your eyes is blood-shot, use my Ring to't,
> They say 'tis very soveraigne.
>
> (I. i. 463–4)

The wedding-ring is destined to bring death in its train. Similarly, the Duchess, feigning to dismiss Antonio:

> You had the tricke, in Audit time to be sicke,
> Till I had sign'd your *Quietus*; and that cur'de you
> Without help of a Doctor.
>
> (III. ii. 223–5)

Other points given prominence in *The White Devil* are repeated.
Pills as poison, for instance: 'why do'st thou wrap thy poysond
Pilles/In Gold, and Sugar?' (IV. i. 23–4) Physic is a purgative:

> *Ferdinand.*   Rubarbe, oh, for rubarbe
>   To purge this choller—
>   (II. v. 18–19)

But this measure, if unsuccessful, must be pursued more sternly:

> *Ferdinand.*   Apply desperate physike—
>   We must not now use Balsamum, but fire,
>   The smarting cupping-glasse, for that's the meane
>   To purge infected blood.
>   (II. v. 33–6)

Blood-letting, the simplest form of symbolism for death, is an
idea that Webster takes seriously, by no means a cliché. The
last word on the subject is Bosola's 'blacke deedes must be
cur'de with death' (V. iv. 45). Here, the implications of 'cur'de'
are much more important than the resemblance to Seneca's 'Per
scelera semper sceleribus tutum est iter.' Bosola's saying seems
to summarize Webster's position on this subject; the futility of
all remedies save death for human ills is a consistent thought.

It is a thought again reinforced by the very obvious distrust
with which Webster views physicians. As before, this distrust
emerges in the plot. Ferdinand's doctor is a fool. Glib, con-
ceited, and misguided, he is first cousin to Webster's lawyers;
and he figures in a scene of black comedy wherein his aping of
Ferdinand's tricks meets with rapid retribution: 'there's nothing
left of you, but tongue, and belly, flattery, and leachery' (v. ii.
79–80).

Thus, passages such as

> *Duchess.*   This puts me in minde of death, Physitians thus,
>   With their hands full of money, use to give ore
>   Their Patients.
>   (III. v. 11–13)

together with I. i. 250–2 and II. i. 42–5, can be regarded as
satirist's material: bitter, highly charged, but not necessarily
tragic. It must be set alongside the philosopher's attitude.
Bosola concludes his meditation

all our feare,
(Nay all our terrour) is, least our Phisition
Should put us in the ground, to be made sweete.

(II. i. 60–2)

Now this whole passage exhibits a crucial switch of mood. Bosola has been railing at Castruchio and the Old Lady in stock satirical terms. His meditation—delivered in verse, not prose— marks the transition from satirist to philosopher. It is an elegy for humanity. Man, bestial, corrupt, and disease-ridden, must submit to the one certain cure. The mechanisms of the universe must supply the remedy to the sickness of humanity. This, too, emerges from Ferdinand's 'Intemperate agues, make Physitians cruell' (IV. i. 170). Ferdinand of course sees himself as the phys- ician. But as the play unfolds this saying takes on two further meanings. Ironically, it looks forward to the scene when the Doctor is cruel to him: 'I'll buffet his madnesse out of him' (v. ii. 27). And Ferdinand becomes a fragment of the play's larger meaning; a sufferer from the 'ague' that is life, he must share the common remedy of humanity.

That remedy, death, is seen as a process in itself, rather than a means employed by a Higher Physician. Webster does not seek to impose an identity upon the activating forces of the universe. Elsewhere it is plain that Webster's vision is of a universe with- out God. It is the symbolism of the process that fascinates him.

It is Webster's attitude towards physicians, as much as any other single feature of his work, that inclines me to doubt the claim that 'Webster, in two plays, made the satiric voice co- equal with the tragic.'[36] Certainly in a few passages one might take Webster's view of physicians, as of lawyers, to be purely satiric. But the final position is utterly different; the satiric voice has been overwhelmed in the tragic. Physic and law move from literal to symbolic. In the last act of *The Duchess of Malfi* the failure of the doctors is not a failure of society, but of humanity. The perspective has widened beyond that of Jacobean England. The ills that Webster diagnoses 'are from eternity, and shall not fail'.

The goal to which all the images of the body point is death. Those images that directly mention, or very broadly symbolize, the idea of death are many—some fifty, by my count. They are,

[36] Bogard, op. cit., p. 5.

however, no more than the crystallization of the far greater num-
bers of images that imply death. To images of the body one can
add war, shadow, winter, tragedy, ruins, echoes. All are deeply
impregnated with the idea of death. And what is expressed in
words, is manifest in the action. The greater part of the action
takes place at night; the ruins present a visual symbol of doomed
humanity; the plot is an almost unrelieved procession of death.
Delio, the Horatio figure, is the irreducible minimum reserved
for the closing speech. All the others have met the fate fore-
shadowed in the imagery.

This fate is realized quite consistently. The act of dying is
depicted as an event of pain and horror: 'their death, a hideous
storme of terror' (IV. ii. 191). But the state of death evokes a
quite different range of ideas. The passages occurring towards
the end collectively represent a concept of death:

> Bosola.   A long war disturb'd your minde,
>   Here your perfect peace is sign'd—
>
>   (IV. ii. 186–7)
> Duchess.   Come violent death,
>   Serve for *Mandragora*, to make me sleepe;
>
>   (IV. ii. 241–2)
> Servant.   Where are you Sir?
> Antonio.   Very neere my home:
>
>   (V. iv. 58–9)

Peace; sleep; cure; home; rest: once the pain of dying is over,
these are the symbols that beckon Webster's characters into the
mist. From this side of the void death represents, not horror—
I find in *The Duchess of Malfi* nothing of the necrophilist psychopath of legend—but ease, rest, home. To seek higher pleasures is
to 'vault credit'. The last word I leave, not with Webster, but
with Spenser, who a generation before had expressed most of
what Webster has to say here:

> Sleepe after toyle, port after stormie seas,
> Ease after warre, death after life does greatly please.
>
>   (*Faerie Queene*, I. ix. 40–1)

The death images round off this survey of the images of corruption and the body; and it is worth making a formal summary of
the ideas associated with them. The body images have the
strongest links with the animal imagery, and on numerous oc-

casions state or imply that man is kin to the beasts. Viewed in its own right the body is seen as, above all, mortal. The body itself is dead or dying; in action it alternates between frenetic violence and sick malfunction. Paralysis, fever, disease, and pain constitute its normal state. Physic and physicians are equally useless. Omnipresent is death; and the transition from death in life to death is seen as a release, and an easement of pain.

The Duchess of Malfi presents a subtler (though comparable) statement on evil than that made in *The White Devil*. The weight has shifted from the explicit to the implicit. That is to say, there are fewer references to 'devils' and 'politic' (the Machiavellian code-word). The play has its devil-possessed and Machiavellian characters, but they do not present the central problems. They do, however, embody Webster's clearest apprehension of evil: that state, or action, in which appearance is opposed to reality. From this derives the conclusion that the Duchess's sin lies in choosing a path in which appearance and reality are divorced— a sort of incompetent Machiavellianism. Mortality itself is a state of inner corruption concealed under a fair surface; and through the many images of the body and its ills, allied with those of animals, Webster makes a sustained and powerful suggestion that mankind is inherently corrupt. In a sense, therefore, I agree with Mr. Bogard that the theme of *The Duchess of Malfi* is 'natural evil'.[37] But Webster's apprehension of evil is imaginative, not theological. Damnation, the theological outcome of evil, does not on the evidence of *The Duchess of Malfi* interest him. The symbols of mortal evil that capture Webster's imagination hold their significance for this world, not the next.

2. THE LAW

Service and payment, reward and punishment are again vital to the argument. In the earlier play the idea was presented through the progresses of four characters; here it is expressed almost entirely through the relationship between Bosola and Ferdinand. (The exceptions are few. Antonio speaks of never taking wages of virtue (I. i. 504–5): he is dismissed complaining of the 'inconstant, /And rotten ground of service' (III. ii. 235–6). Julia dies speaking of 'Justice' (v. ii. 308), an ironic parallel to 'Salary

[37] Ibid., p. 133.

for his Lust' (v. i. 58).) Ferdinand stands nominally for the
Law; Bosola is the instrument of Ferdinand, dominated by the
thought of payment for his services: together they set up a
dialogue that probes the implications of the law metaphor. The
images occur, with one exception, in the crucial areas of the exposition, the final act, and the passage immediately following the
Duchess's death.

The theme is stated at once. Bosola is hardly on stage before
he is growling to the Cardinal: 'I have done you better service
then to be slighted thus: miserable age, where onely the reward
of doing well, is the doing of it!' (i. i. 32–4) To Antonio and
Delio he complains: 'There are rewards for hawkes, and dogges,
when they have done us service; but for a Souldier, that hazards
his Limbes in a battaile, nothing but a kind of Geometry, is his
last Supportation' (i. i. 59–62). This is remarkably reminiscent
of Lodovico. And as before, Webster goes out of his way to
emphasize that the reward is just—Bosola, like Lodovico, has
committed murder (i. i. 71).

The theme extends to Ferdinand. In the character-sketch
which is the plainest indication of Webster's intentions, Delio
and Antonio discuss him thus:

Antonio.   He speakes with others Tongues, and heares mens
                   suites,
               With others Eares: will seeme to sleepe o'th bench
               Onely to intrap offenders, in their answeres;
               Doombes men to death, by information,
               Rewards, by heare-say.
Delio.   Then the Law to him
               Is like a fowle blacke cob-web, to a Spider—
               He makes it his dwelling, and a prison
               To entangle those shall feede him.
Antonio.   Most true:
               He nev'r paies debts, unlesse they be shrewd turnes,
               And those he will confesse that he doth owe.
                                              (i. i. 175–86)

So Ferdinand's actions constitute a massive denial of law. Bosola,
in his quest for justice, has given himself over to one who per-
verts justice.

The theme is allowed to lapse in the middle of the play.

Once only does Webster permit himself an ironic image, of the type he loves. Bosola, flattering the Duchess, asserts

> For know an honest states-man to a Prince,
> Is like a Cedar, planted by a Spring,
> The Spring bathes the trees roote, the gratefull tree
> Rewards it with his shadow: you have not done so—
>
> (III. ii. 303–6)

He deceives not only the Duchess but himself. He is the 'honest states-man', or servant, to the Prince; the reward he seeks is denied him.

The full import of the situation is revealed when Ferdinand and Bosola confront each other across the Duchess's corpse. This is the *anagnorisis* of the drama: the truth for Ferdinand is the realization that he has murdered the one he loves, for Bosola that he has committed murder in vain. For both the issue is justice. Their dialogue, a sustained series of legal metaphors, has all the brilliance of a clash of first-class barristers in court:

Bosola.	Let me quicken your memory: for I perceive
	You are falling into ingratitude: I challenge
	The reward due to my service.
Ferdinand.	I'll tell thee,
	What I'll give thee—
Bosola.	Doe:
Ferdinand.	I'll give thee a pardon
	For this murther:
Bosola.	Hah?
Ferdinand.	Yes: and 'tis
	The largest bounty I can studie to doe thee.
	By what authority did'st thou execute
	This bloody sentence?
Bosola.	By yours—
Ferdinand.	Mine? was I her Judge?
	Did any ceremoniall forme of Law,
	Doombe her to not-Being? did a compleat Jury
	Deliver her conviction up i'th Court?
	Where shalt thou find this judgement registerd
	Unlesse in hell? See: like a bloody foole
	Th'hast forfeyted thy life, and thou shalt die for't.
Bosola.	The Office of Justice is perverted quite
	When one Thiefe hangs another: who shall dare
	To reveale this?

Ferdinand.	Oh, I'll tell thee:
	The Wolfe shall finde her Grave, and scrape it up:
	Not to devour the corpes, but to discover
	The horrid murther.
Bosola.	You; not I, shall quake for't.
Ferdinand.	Leave me:
Bosola.	I will first receive my Pention.
Ferdinand.	You are a villaine:
Bosola.	When your Ingratitude
	Is Judge, I am so.
Ferdinand.	O horror!
	That not the feare of him, which bindes the divels
	Can prescribe man obedience.
	Never looke upon me more.

(IV. ii. 311–43)

The central metaphor of the Law has several aspects. Ferdinand rejects his status under human law, and appeals to the morality of a higher law. Bosola appeals to a simple law of contract. Webster, the master ironist, indicates that there is a law of retribution that dooms them both. The mechanisms of the universe—the playwright does not ask us to term them the 'Divine Law'—bring disappointment, followed by death, for the one; and madness, followed by death, for the other. In that sense, justice is done, and seen to be done. The fourth act of *The Duchess of Malfi* contains a miniature court scene that completes the triptych of trial scenes in his three plays.

The final scenes present the culmination of the theme. The antics of the demented Ferdinand evoke Bosola's awed comment:

> Mercy upon me, what a fatall judgement
> Hath falne upon this *Ferdinand*!
>
> (v. ii. 83–4)

The scene ends with Bosola vowing:

> It may be,
> I'll joyne with thee, in a most just revenge.
> The weakest Arme is strong enough, that strikes
> With the sword of Justice . . .
>
> (v. ii. 377–80)

Revenge, for Webster, is bound up with justice; indeed, I should not care to term Webster's plays as revenge tragedies except in the sense of dramatizations of Bacon's 'Revenge is a kind of wild justice.' Justice becomes explicitly the issue of the last scene. To the Cardinal Bosola says:

> when thou kill'dst thy sister,
> Thou tookst from Justice her most equall ballance,
> And left her naught but her sword.
>
> (v. v. 52–5)

Once the instrument of a false justice, Bosola conceives himself the means of enforcing true justice; and this the Cardinal admits with his dying

> Oh Justice:
> I suffer now, for what hath former bin:
> "Sorrow is held the eldest child of sin.
>
> (v. v. 72–4)

As he kills Ferdinand, Bosola restates the theme, combining 'revenge' with 'service':

> Now my revenge is perfect: sinke (thou maine cause
> Of my undoing)—the last part of my life,
> Hath done me best service.
>
> (v. v. 81–3)

In Bosola's end is his beginning. He must abide the faintly mocking comment of the dying Cardinal: 'Thou hast thy payment too' (v. v. 93). He has opened the play asking for payment, and he closes the play receiving it. What remains is a formal chord restating the idea:

> *Roderigo.*   How comes this?
> *Bosola.*   Revenge, for the Duchesse of *Malfy*, murdred
>   By th' Aragonian brethren: for *Antonio*,
>   Slaine by this hand: for lustfull *Julia*,
>   Poyson'd by this man: and lastly, for my selfe . . .
>
> (v. v. 101–5)

True justice remains Bosola's final thought:

> Let worthy mindes nere stagger in distrust
> To suffer death, or shame, for what is just—
>
> (v. v. 127–8)

Justice has many faces. The Law, revenge, service, payment are some of them: they all contribute to a concept central to *The*

Duchess of Malfi, one that can reasonably be described as the Law. The metaphor covers earthly law; the moral law, to which both Ferdinand and Bosola refer; and the law of retribution, which condemns them, and all the other actors.

Retribution is not so dominant a concern with the Webster of *The Duchess of Malfi*. The point that sin brings its own reward is not one that needs to be reiterated endlessly. Accordingly, the focus of the tragic issues is shared by Bosola, the Duchess, Antonio. The *hamartia* of Antonio is ambition; of the Duchess, a madness, 'a lust of the blood and a permission of the will'; of Bosola, an intellectual failure to apprehend his personal identity and his responsibility for his actions. And all these forms of sin, and error, are implicitly affected by the play's images of corruption and animality. The overwhelming weight of suggestion is that it is mankind's fate to sin, that the corruption of the body will manifest itself in corrupt action. The drift towards error, and its consequent calling into being of the mechanisms of retribution, is in great part the meaning of *The Duchess of Malfi*. But something else remains. The human mind, confronted with the body's tendencies, has yet a responsibility for the actions of the body. The exercise of that responsibility is the subject of a prolonged and searching examination by Webster in his second tragedy, growing out of a slighter treatment of the matter in *The White Devil*. The philosophy that emerges from his analysis of responsibility is what we have now to consider.

3. KNOWLEDGE

The third major theme of *The Duchess of Malfi* is the problem of knowledge. I call it that, because the theme is conveyed *inter alia* in the significant repetitions of the verb 'to know'. But the nature of this theme demands a broad approach. It raises the whole question of the philosophy dramatized in the play. For that philosophy we need a name; and when one comes to hand we need not hesitate to use it. The term best adapted to describe—not define—the philosophy expressed in *The Duchess of Malfi* is existentialism.

Existentialism, as a conscious and identifiable philosophical concern, dates from the nineteenth century. It therefore seems at best an academic exercise to search for traces of it in the remoter past. Nevertheless, a strong case can on occasion be mounted for such a search. Sartre himself recognized Pascal, certain other seventeenth-century French philosophers, and the pessimists of the classical era as legitimate precursors.[38] It is hardly as a philosophical tradition, however, that I wish to approach it here. Kaufmann's approach seems to me the most useful one: 'Existentialism is a timeless sensibility that can be discerned here and there in the past; but it is only in recent times that it has hardened into a sustained protest and preoccupation.'[39] When a writer exhibits this sensibility to a marked extent, we can properly approach him through our understanding of a contemporary philosophy.

What are the elements of this 'timeless sensibility'? No standard formulation exists, but I shall adopt Edmund Wilson's concise summary. Existentialism, he says,

places man in a world without God (though not all existentialists are atheists) in which all the moral values are developed by man himself . . . Man is free, beyond certain limits, to choose what he is to be and to do. His life has significance solely in its relation to the lives of others—in his actions or refraining from action: to use a phrase of Sartre's, the individual must 'engage himself'.[40]

Clearly, such a world view—in a generalized, not in its modern and rigorous form—can often be encountered in the past. It is particularly relevant to the early seventeenth century, a period which has often afforded parallels with the twentieth century. More precisely, Shakespeare has been claimed as a forerunner of existentialism. Kaufmann has argued for this view of Shakespeare: 'He knew the view that man is thrown into the world, abandoned to a life that ends in death, with nothing after that; but he also knew self-sufficiency.'[41] For Kaufmann, Prospero's final speech is the clearest illustration of this. Again, 'Sartre's world is closer to Shakespeare's.'[42] More recently, David Horo-

[38] J.-P. Sartre, 'An Explication of *The Stranger*', in *Camus*, ed. Germaine Brée (Prentice-Hall, Englewood Cliffs, N.J., 1962), p. 109.

[39] Walter Kaufmann, *Existentialism from Dostoevsky to Sartre* (Meridian, New York, 1956), p. 12.

[40] Edmund Wilson, 'Jean-Paul Sartre: The Novelist and the Existentialist', in *Sartre*, ed. Edith Kern (Prentice-Hall, Englewood Cliffs, N.J., 1962), p. 49.

[41] Walter Kaufmann, *The Owl and the Nightingale* (Beacon Press, Boston, Mass., 1959), p. 3.

[42] Kaufmann, *Existentialism from Dostoevsky to Sartre*, p. 47.

witz has published an existentialist analysis of Shakespeare.[43] In the case of Webster, however, I know only of one or two hints. Ornstein mentions the possibility, only to reject it, that 'I am Duchess of Malfi still' is an existentialist statement.[44] Miss Bradbrook has since then thrown out some broad hints that we could profitably look at Webster in the light of our knowledge of existentialism. 'The "absurd", incongruous conjunction of adverse circumstances in Webster could be paralleled in Sartre or Camus.'[45] They can, indeed. We can, however, go much further than this, and examine not only the concept of the absurd, but other central existentialist motifs that occur in Webster, most notably in *The Duchess of Malfi*. The evidence that Webster possessed to a remarkable extent this 'timeless sensibility' is very considerable.

We can dispose first of generalities. There are certain broad similarities between the concerns of Webster and of our contemporary existentialists that have only to be named. First, there is a universe which is, in effect, without God. I do not mean by this that Webster was himself an atheist. As a private person, he does not concern us; we consider only the Webster who is the author of three plays. And the crude gestures associated with overt atheism in the recent Elizabethan past were only to be avoided by a dramatist of any sensibility. Nevertheless, the two tragedies, especially the second, can only be read as explorations of a universe that is without God. The Duchess of Malfi can die in the expressed hope of heaven. For all the other major characters, the only certainty is the self, and beyond that the unfathomable void. The balance of dramatic suggestion lies overwhelmingly with Flamineo's 'Noe, at my selfe I will begin and end' and Bosola's 'I'll be mine owne example.' The positive values are human, not religious. No extra-subjective reality is seriously advanced.

Second, there is the common concern with the absurd. Sartre has written,

[43] David Horowitz, *Shakespeare: An Existentialist View* (Tavistock Press, London, 1965). 'By "existential", however, I mean simply a view that proves itself in the reality of lived existence, not in the principles of metaphysical or theological discourse' (p. ix).

[44] Robert Ornstein, *The Moral Vision of Jacobean Tragedy* (University of Wisconsin Press, Madison, Wis., 1960), p. 148.

[45] M. C. Bradbrook, *English Dramatic Form* (Chatto and Windus, 1965), p.103.

Primary absurdity manifests a cleavage, the cleavage between man's aspirations to unity and the insurmountable dualism of mind and nature, between man's drive toward the eternal and the *finite* character of his existence, between the 'concern' which constitutes his very essence and the vanity of his efforts. Chance, death, the irreducible pluralism of life and of truth, the unintelligibility of the real—all these are extremes of the absurd.[46]

On one level, this concept is best illustrated in Bosola's 'Looke you, the Starres shine still', which might have been written for the first part of Sartre's explanation. On another level, we can see as the prime absurdity the ceaseless ironies of the action. The reversals of appearance and reality, intention and effect, lead up to Bosola's 'We are meerely the Starres tennys-balls (strooke, and banded/Which way please them)'. Dramatically, Webster's plots are a sustained and subtle series of *peripeteia*. Philosophically, his most mature play accepts the personal limits of knowledge.

And thirdly, there is the question of death. Here Webster is a special case. Every Jacobean tragedy contains death, on stage; it is an obvious theatrical opportunity for speeches dwelling on the meaning of existence. It is agreed that Webster takes these opportunities to a degree far beyond his contemporaries. It is certainly more than a succession of fine theatrical moments, and more than an acquaintance with the tradition that 'truth sits upon the lips of dying men'. It is an awareness that in the hour of defeat man can discover and assert his own identity. The point is familiar to the existentialists: Guicharnaud, for example, has written of Sartre's plays: 'As death is the situation par excellence for bringing man's being into question, whether the tragedy be private or collective, to kill or be killed is the symbol of man's greatest problem.'[47]

We can conveniently illustrate the idea here from *The White Devil* and *The Devil's Law-Case*. Lodovico and Flamineo most exactly define themselves in death. Lodovico's essential gesture is to reject not only society's laws, but also the moral values that society accepts in principle. Lodovico will not accept that a society that can tolerate the Duke of Brachiano cannot find place for him. He is a creature of appetite, purely; he wants Isabella,

[46] Sartre, 'An Explication of *The Stranger*', *Camus*, p. 109.
[47] Jacques Guicharnaud, 'Man and his Acts', in *Sartre*, p. 64.

he will revenge himself on Brachiano and Flamineo. And yet this
'thing of blood' has his values, his integrity. He is a professional.
The penultimate scene (v. v) reveals him pressing his master
Francisco not to endanger himself. He himself has paid off his
creditors, as a man should. A spark of reciprocal feeling comes
from his master, and Francisco finds a word to reassure his
hireling:

> If thou do'st perish in this glorious act,
> Ile reare unto thy memorie that fame
> Shall in the ashes keepe alive thy name.
>
> (v. v. 9–11)

This is a strange promise. Yet it is not intended as mere rhetoric.
'Fame' is not an irrelevant appendage to death; the foreknowledge of it serves as a personal satisfaction *during life*. This is the
point, for Lodovico. Francisco gives, and Lodovico is meant to
receive, a promise that has some meaning in the perilous passage
to come. That this is so, is confirmed by Lodovico himself at the
last:

> I do glory yet,
> That I can call this act mine owne: For my part,
> The racke, the gallowes, and the torturing wheele
> Shall bee but sound sleepes to me, here's my rest—
> "I limb'd this night-peece and it was my best.
>
> (v. vi. 295–9)

To call this act 'mine owne' is for Lodovico the highest expression of his philosophy. The deed was well worth accomplishing,
and professionally executed. The penalties of the Law Lodovico
accepts with total equanimity. It is the final gesture of a genu-
inely existentialist figure. For Lodovico, as for Meursault, the
brutalities of the end cannot disturb the individual's triumphant
realization of himself. 'For all to be accomplished, for me to feel
less lonely, all that remained was to hope that on the day of my
execution there should be a large crowd of spectators and that
they should greet me with howls of execration' (*The Outsider*).

Flamineo's is a character of greater complexity. Its structure
is however made perfectly plain, through the motivation speech
of I. ii. 308–25. Flamineo has allowed himself to be defined by
economic necessity. There are hints that service runs counter to

his preference, but Flamineo is no innocent corrupted; it is not service that compels him to kill his brother. The overriding impression one receives of Flamineo is that of a man eager for sensation, for new truths and experiences. This operates on several levels. There is the *voyeurisme*[48] with which he observes the coupling of Brachiano and Vittoria. Then there is the detached, intellectual curiosity of the scholar on meeting Brachiano's ghost: 'Pray, Sir, resolve mee, what religions best/For a man to die in?' (v. iv. 122–3). Finally, he is interested in, but imperfectly conscious of, himself. It is the only value, and he comes to it at the end. Morally, he is rudderless. The temporal goal of his activity lies in ruins. He is going to die very shortly. The fundamental question has to be faced after all. Lodovico asks it: 'What dost thinke on?' (v. vi. 202)

It is a good question: not so good as the even more fundamental question that the Duchess is to put via Bosola to herself, 'Who am I?' But it is certainly the most probing question in a play of few questions. For what *can* Flamineo think on? The immediate answer has a tremendous philosophical weight: 'Nothing; of nothing.' The negative carries with it a rejection of all dogma, all formula. Nor is there any whining repentance, which could be only a last-minute acceptance of other men's doctrines. The real answer comes a moment later:

> I doe not looke
> Who went before, nor who shall follow mee;
> Noe, at my selfe I will begin and end.
>
> (v. vi. 256–8)

It is the most perfect existentialist statement in Webster. The individual consciousness is its own justification; realizing and asserting it is the life value. And what is the type of consciousness that Flamineo asserts at the end? It is that of the actor. Not the actor who acts another part, but the actor who *is*, in acting. We can justify this statement with two metaphors, besides the attitude struck in Flamineo's dying words. Near the end, Flamineo employs two actor's images: 'I am ith way to study a long silence' (v. vi. 204) and 'I have lost my voice/Most irrecoverably'

---

[48] A hint, perhaps, of the concealed incest of *The Duchess of Malfi*. But Flamineo, far from resisting (as does Ferdinand) the sexual mating of his sister, is happy to identify with Brachiano.

(v. vi. 271–2). And there is the quite definite consciousness of striking a pose in his final lines:

> Let no harsh flattering Bels resound my knell,
> Strike thunder, and strike lowde to my farewell.
>
> (v. vi. 275–6)

It is a superb final curtain, and Flamineo knows it. Clifford Leech, who has well described Flamineo's capacity for observing, and standing outside himself, writes that Flamineo 'rallies his forces and exults that at the last he has spoken his words well'.[49] I should prefer to take these words not as a metaphorical comment, but as a statement of actuality. Flamineo at the last *is* an actor; or, if one prefers, a *poseur*, a man for whom striking attitudes is existence.

The Devil's Law-Case presents a late crystallization of the idea. Romelio, on the brink of a duel, is confronted with the Capuchin's endeavours at late conversion:

Romelio.	Who has hired you to make me Coward?
Capuchin.	I would make you
	A good Christian.
Romelio.	Withall, let me continue
	An honest man, which I am very certaine,
	A coward can never be:

> (v. iv. 74–9)

'Honesty' here, as in *The Duchess of Malfi*, refers to the 'integrity of life' that is the ultimate Websterian value; and its parallel is with Meursault's rejection of the priest at the close of *The Outsider*.

In general terms, then, Webster's plays reveal areas of concern that coincide with those of the twentieth-century existentialists. Our special concern here, however, is *The Duchess of Malfi*. Within the framework discussed above, Webster elaborates a study of the existentialist position. It can conveniently be analysed under two heads: as a philosophical theme centred on the problem of knowledge, and as a matter specific to Bosola and the Duchess.

(a) The Problem of Knowledge

Unlike that of *The White Devil*, the atmosphere of *The Duchess of Malfi* is charged with doubt and questionings. At different times,

---

[49] Leech, op. cit., p. 52.

all the characters are racked with doubt as to the meaning of life, and the rightness of their course through it. Constantly they ask each other questions, and receive from one another inconclusive answers. Throughout the play the words 'know', and 'knowledge' recur steadily.

Purely on a level of imagery, this theme is sustained in several ways. There are some score of images of science, learning, and reading. The stars suggest the bounds of knowledge (as well as fate), and astrologers and intelligencers symbolize the quest for knowledge. The matter cannot be examined in a restrictive way, however, and the approach must be widened to include imagery, plot, characterization, and the literal text.

It is convenient to begin with an aspect of Bosola. Like Flamineo, he turns out to be an alumnus of Padua. The choice of this university is worth more space than it is normally accorded in editions of Webster. Padua was a famous seat of humanist learning; Galileo's university, it had a European reputation for advanced and speculative thinking. The visitor can still view the anatomical theatre—built in 1594, the first in Europe—in which one can conceive some prototypical Bosola attending anatomy lectures, 'to teach man/Wherein hee is imperfect . . .' This environment helps to fix Bosola, and Delio elaborates the picture:

> I knew him in *Padua*, a fantasticall scholler,
> Like such, who studdy to know how many knots
> Was in *Hercules* club, of what colour *Achilles* beard was,
> Or whether *Hector* were not troubled with the tooth-ach—
> He hath studdied himselfe halfe bleare-ei'd, to know
> The true semitry of *Caesars* nose by a shooing-horne,
> And this he did
> To gaine the name of a speculative man.
>
> (III. iii. 50-7)

This 'carracter' (none the less important for its irony) comes rather oddly, and late in III. iii. Its natural place is in the exposition: doubtless Webster felt that the audience had as many 'carracters' as it could take in the opening scene. At all events, he goes out of his way here to insist on Bosola's reputation as a restless, even fantastical seeker after knowledge. But this is not only his undergraduate persona, it is his dramatic function. As Ferdinand's intelligencer, Bosola's role is to acquire knowledge for his master. The trade of spying parodies the quest for knowledge. Bosola, then, is a spy and a scholar. And his main interest, of central significance to himself and the play as a whole, is astrology.

Astrology first occurs in Act II. Bosola has the jargon at his finger-tips: 'Oh (Sir) you are Lord of the ascendant, chiefe man with the Duchesse, a Duke was your cosen German, remov'd' (II. i. 99–100). This hint is strengthened in the horoscope scene when Antonio asserts that he has been 'setting a figure' for the Duchess's jewels. Bosola immediately responds with the code-words of the expert:

> Ah: and how falls your question?
> Doe you find it radicall?
> > (II. iii. 29–30)

He has no trouble in making immediate sense of the horoscope which Antonio lets slip: 'Why now 'tis most apparant' (II. iii. 81)—though it would hardly be so to any but one thoroughly versed in the mystery.

Of all the earthly sciences, astrology is the most ambitious. It seeks some, at least, of the answers to terrestrial problems in extra-terrestrial terms. To the Jacobeans, making no distinction between our 'astronomy' and 'astrology', the study represented the uttermost frontier of human knowledge; and the ferment of the years following Galileo's discovery made the symbol peculiarly potent. As the play proceeds, the astrology motif grows in significance. The Cardinal touches on it ironically, in his scene with Julia:

> We had need goe borrow that fantastique glasse
> Invented by *Galileo* the Florentine,
> To view another spacious world i'th'Moone,
> And looke to find a constant woman there.
> > (II. iv. 24–7)

Far more important is the passage between Bosola and his employer:

Ferdinand. Now *Bosola,*
How thrives our intelligence?
Bosola. (Sir) uncertainly—
'Tis rumour'd she hath had three bastards, but
By whom, we may go read i'th'Starres.

Ferdinand.   Why some
                Hold opinion, all things are written there.
Bosola.   Yes, if we could find Spectacles to read them—

(III. i. 69–76)

There is a certain luminous quality in this passage. The meaning
extends far beyond the literal sense of the text. 'Intelligence'
here suggests something profounder than acts of petty spying;
reading the stars is more than a glib conversational topic of contemporary interest. The theme is knowledge; the implication,
failure. Bosola does not have the spectacles.

The same implication is present in the crucial dialogue between Bosola and the Duchess in Act IV:

Duchess.   I could curse the Starres.
Bosola.   Oh fearefull!
Duchess.   And those three smyling seasons of the yeare
               Into a Russian winter: nay the world
               To its first Chaos.
Bosola.   Looke you, the Starres shine still.

(IV. i. 115–20)

An exact interpretation of this passage cannot be advanced.
'Looke you, the Starres shine still' belongs to that order of lines,
like 'Et in Arcadia ego', which must be interpreted by the reader
after his own fashion. Lucas saw in it a sublime cynicism, expressing 'the insignificance of human agony before the impassive
Universe'.[50] The actor's delivery could assume a tone of scepticism, cynicism, sadness, even consolation. The stars, I believe,
generate diverse symbolic values here. They suggest ineluctable
fate; and man's baffled quest for knowledge. As such, they take
up the Ferdinand-Bosola dialogue previously quoted.

And astrology figures in the ensuing scene. One of the madmen is

an Astrologian,
That in his workes, sayd such a day o'th'moneth
Should be the day of doome: and fayling of't,
Ran mad:

(IV. ii. 51–4)

A little later this madman cries: 'Doomes-day not come yet? I'll
draw it neerer by a perspective, or make a glasse, that shall set

[50] Lucas, ii. 179.

all the world on fire upon an instant' (IV. ii. 77–9). 'Perspective'
means telescope, according to Lucas;[51] Brown gives it more
broadly as 'optical instrument, magnifying glass'.[52] The broader
term is more useful to my argument here, since I may then regard 'perspective' as a generic term that takes up the earlier
reference to 'spectacles' in the Ferdinand-Bosola passage. In
any case, the 'perspective' allusion is repeated by Bosola: to
him a guilty conscience is 'a Perspective/That showes us hell'
(IV. ii. 386–7). Webster contrasts the burlesque ravings of the
mad astrologer with the agonized self-awakening of the corrupt
scholar, Bosola. As I have already argued (pages 43–5), the mad
scene presents specific parodies of the characters, hence the mad
astrologer is Bosola's zany. For both, their 'perspectives' provide
a view of hell. Thus the final comment in *The Duchess of Malfi* on
a notable field of human endeavour is ironic, perhaps despairing.

The sciences provide no answer to humanity's questionings.
And the play supplies no reassurance when the questions are
posed in religious or philosophical terms. The Duchess asks
Cariola:

Duchess.   Do'st thou thinke we shall know one another,
             In th'other world?
Cariola.   Yes, out of question.
Duchess.   O that it were possible we might
             But hold some two dayes conference with the dead,
             From them, I should learne somewhat, I am sure
             I never shall know here:
                           (IV. ii. 20–5)

In spite of her burst of confidence towards the end—

             Who would be afraid on't?
             Knowing to meete such excellent company
             In th'other world.
                           (IV. ii. 216–18)

the memory of her earlier doubt is indelible. She has, after all,
asked of Bosola the most fundamental of all questions: 'Who

    51 Ibid., p. 182.
    52 Brown, *The Duchess of Malfi*, p. 120. 'Perspective' as a metaphor for Webster's
dramatic techniques is the subject of Inga-Stina Ewbank's disquisition (one especially rich in ideas), 'Webster's Realism, or, "A Cunning Piece Wrought Perspective"', in *John Webster*, ed. Brian Morris (Ernest Benn, London, 1970), pp.
159–78.

am I?' and the answer he gives is negative: 'Thou art a box of worme-seede', etc. (IV. ii. 122–31). Surely this question and answer contain the core of the play's meaning. Bosola's answer has two parts: the first is traditional, the old *de contemptu mundi* message that the body is corrupt and mortal. The second part is a far more personal statement, a rejection of the medieval corollary that we must look to Heaven for the answer to our mortal predicament. On the contrary, Heaven affords not an answer but a reflection of our questionings. Nowhere more clearly than in this exchange is the existentialism of *The Duchess of Malfi* to be discerned.

Given the limits of knowledge, in what then does human wisdom consist? The matter is raised in the second act when Bosola —for once—is baited concerning his desire for knowledge:

> *Antonio.*   Now Sir, in your contemplation?
>   You are studdying to become a great wise fellow?
> *Bosola.*   Oh Sir, the opinion of wisedom is a foule tettor, that
>   runs all over a mans body: if simplicity direct us to
>   have no evill, it directs us to a happy being: For the
>   subtlest folly proceedes from the subtlest wisedom:
>   Let me be simply honest.
>   (II. i. 79–84)

The drift is clear: book-learning is not wisdom, 'the subtlest folly proceeds from the subtlest wisedome.' Bosola is simply defending himself here, but the course of the play points the accuracy of his parry. For Antonio, 'wisdom' has a different application. The light dialogue with Cariola (III. ii. 41–7) compares his decision with Paris's; it is an equivalent choice of beauty against wisdom. Here wisdom implies the ability to perceive, and achieve the expedient. Antonio, quite simply, makes the wrong choice, an error complementing the Duchess's 'fearfull madnes'. There remains the Cardinal. 'Wisdome begins at the end: remember it', he enjoins the Duchess (I. i. 366). This is a gnomic saying; and the Cardinal's own end is equally gnomic. 'Let me/Be layd by, and never thought of' (V. v. 112–13). Wisdom must consider the final view; but how if that final view is a yielding to oblivion? How can wisdom begin at the end, when the end is unknown?

And so the quest for knowledge, after all, comes back to Bosola's answer: 'the Heaven ore our heades, like her looking glasse, onely gives us a miserable knowledge of the small compasse of our prison' (IV. ii. 129–31). Of all the play's answers, this comes nearest to summarizing the idea Webster wishes to express. In brief, the matter stands thus. Science and scholarship, in the persons of Bosola, the doctor, and the mad astrologer, are tried and found wanting. The philosophy of the Duchess leads to a final affirmation of belief, yet it is preceded by much doubt and questionings. Wisdom may take due note of expediency, but must ultimately reside in 'simple honesty' or 'integrity of life'. It is certainly not the product of 'study'. The final figure-in-action supports the point; one, perhaps, as important as the horoscope scene, which asserts the symbolic significance of astrology. The last scene of all finds the guilt-ridden Cardinal turning to a theological work for assurance. It purports to discuss the nature of hell. And that, too, affords him no sufficient answer: 'Lay him by.' The answer to man's search for knowledge, if there be one, is not supplied by the scholars.

(b) Bosola

So far, we have discussed the concept of knowledge in *The Duchess of Malfi* on the broadest possible basis. That is necessary, for the concept is diffused throughout the play and affects the actions and thought of all the leading characters. We can now concentrate on Bosola, and devote a fairly elaborate analysis to his character and development. In doing so we can usefully employ the ideas, very considerably associated with the existentialists, of identity, self-deception, role-playing, commitment, and choice.

(i) Who is Bosola? He is first presented, in one of those 'carracters' that within their limits are always to be taken as absolute statements, as a malcontent, a

> Court-Gall: yet I observe his rayling
> Is not for simple love of Piety:
> Indeede he rayles at those things which he wants,
> Would be as leacherous, covetous, or proud,
> Bloody, or envious, as any man,
> If he had meanes to be so:
>
> (I. i. 24–9)

He has a prison record, and murder, to add to these stains of character. Yet he is not without some strain of decency, as Antonio insists:

> 'Tis great pitty
> He should be thus neglected—I have heard
> He's very valiant: This foule mellancholly
> Will poyson all his goodnesse.
>
> (I. i. 75–8)

A divided nature, then; a confused identity. And he has to cope with a difficult moral problem, when Ferdinand offers him employment—of a sort. Bosola states the issue very clearly:

> oh, that to avoid ingratitude
> For the good deed you have done me, I must doe
> All the ill man can invent:
>
> (I. i. 297–9)

Bosola has to choose between two courses of action, which involve the opposed values of 'honour' and 'honesty'. 'Honour' is in this play a tainted concept. For Ferdinand and his brother, it is a crazed, inhuman code of family pride. For Bosola, 'honour' is professionalism, the ethic of carrying out one's professional assignment efficiently. It is an idea closely related to the play's images of contract, service, and payment. Yet this professionalism may involve the most degrading duties. 'Honour', therefore, confronts 'honesty', which implies a policy of action consistent with one's own nature. It is noteworthy that 'action' is placed before the audience at the play's beginning—and end. 'Want of action', we are told, is spoiling Bosola (I. i. 81): 'noble action', according to Antonio, is stimulated by horsemanship (I. i. 147). The two references to 'action' are clearly balanced. Bosola, then, chooses a course of action that is ultimately opposed to his inner values. He has imperfectly understood his own identity.

(ii) But what exactly *is* Bosola's identity? It is certainly a start to say that he possesses mixed elements of good and evil. But we have to go much further than this. The most important characteristic of Bosola is that his behaviour is a series of role-playing changes.

(a) The first I have already alluded to, his undergraduate pose of 'fantasticall scholler' at Padua (III. iii. 50–7). According to Delio, he had even then acquired the notoriety of a man who throws himself enthusiastically into the pursuit, or pose, of the

moment. It is a well-known undergraduate act, and on its own
would not merit comment.

(b) It has, however, clearly been changed for the fashionable
adult pose of the day, the melancholic. To be exact, the day before yesterday, as Antonio unkindly tells him:

> Because you would not seeme to appeare to th'world
> Puff'd up with your preferment: You continue
> This out of fashion mellancholly—leave it, leave it.
>
> (II. i. 87–9)

It is not quite clear here whether the pose of the melancholic
man is of his own choosing, or whether Bosola is obeying Ferdinand's behest: 'Be your selfe:/Keepe your old garbe of melen-
cholly' (I. i. 302–3). It is clear, however, that both as intellectual
and as melancholic, Bosola acts out his roles well. It seems to
satisfy some inner desire in him. Both the process of acting,
and the essence of the parts, seem to express him.

(c) The third role is his professional function, that of bravo
and spy. Here again Bosola is exceptionally competent in the
discharge of his duties. Moreover, his work involves a further
degree of acting: in particular, the business of the apricot trick,
and the unctuous virtue with which, descanting on Antonio's
merits, he induces the Duchess to blurt out the truth.

(d) A certain talent for acting, for seizing on and carrying
out the niceties of behaviour appropriate to a role, emerges from
all this. It becomes more subtly apparent in the prolonged torture of the Duchess in Act IV. Here we see a development in
Bosola's character not dissimilar to Flamineo's, that of the
voyeur, the aesthete, the observer. Bosola becomes a connoisseur
of suffering; he provides a number of different emotional stimuli
to the Duchess—doom, hope, admonition, consolation, question
and answer. He becomes a sort of stooge, feeding the Duchess in
all manner of ways, so that she can better express the precise
nature of her situation.

(e) The role-playing becomes formalized in the later stages of
the Duchess's torture. Bosola, sickened by it all, absolutely de-
clines to continue in his own shape:

> Never in mine owne shape,
> That's forfeited, by my intelligence,
> And this last cruell lie:
>
> (IV. i. 161–3)

He presides over the final stages of the execution dressed as an old man: he announces his identity to be first a tombmaker, then a bellman: "'Twas to bring you/By degrees to mortification' (IV. ii. 178–9). He does not, in fact, reveal his identity as 'Bosola' again to the Duchess. And so Bosola acts out the final charade of the execution. This has a ceremonial, elegiac aspect; it is preceded by the lament, 'Hearke, now every thing is still', and the death of the Duchess is at least partly presented as a foreshortening of a natural, mortal process. This accomplished, Bosola instantly reassumes the role of the professional. The cynical, determined efficiency of his disposal of Cariola is in complete contrast to his despatching of the Duchess. The man who can say 'Why then,/Your credit's sav'd' (IV. ii. 268–9) is playing a quite different role from the compassionate ancient, whispering of mortality, who presides over the dissolution of the Duchess. Indeed, the break is sharp, instantaneous; Bosola, as soon as the Duchess is strangled, raps out the orders that will finish the business:

> Where's the waiting woman?
> Fetch her: Some other strangle the children:
>
> (IV. ii. 245–6)

What emerges from all this is the variety of roles that Bosola plays. Intellectual, melancholic, spy and assassin, tombmaker and bellman, causer and observer of death—he plays them all; and it is at least partly true of Bosola, as of Flamineo, that in acting he is expressing himself. And it is strongly suggested, in his dying words, that he sees himself in this light. It is true that an ambiguity attaches itself to the word 'actor':

> for my selfe,
> (That was an Actor in the maine of all,
> Much 'gainst mine owne good nature, yet i'th'end
> Neglected.)
> (V. v. 105–8)

'Actor' may mean, neutrally, a 'doer', or can refer specifically to the stage. But the word is surely given positive colouring by the image Bosola employs a moment later: 'Such a mistake, as I have often seene/In a play' (V. v. 119–20). Always, at the point of death, it is the things which matter most that Webster's characters speak of. The essence that is Bosola is expressed in acting.

(iii) But there is more yet to sift. Bosola himself believes that there is a 'good nature' that is opposed to, and presumably separate from, the roles he enacts. This view is implicitly accepted by C. G. Thayer, who comments: 'the symbolic throwing-off of the disguise must certainly mean that the actor has become the man, that instead of acting out further the role of Ferdinand's creature or the role of a vicious malcontent, he will now abide by his own principles.'[53] We have now to scrutinize this belief; and we shall do so sceptically, having already indicated that it is not possible to separate 'actor' (in either sense) from the 'man'. The question has to be put to Bosola: why, if indeed he possesses a 'good nature', does he engage voluntarily in the trade of spy and assassin, knowing it to be against his nature?

It is the fundamental question hereabouts, made sharper by the knowledge that Bosola's actual professional competence is in no way reduced by his scruples. His contractual obligations are discharged with the utmost rigour, by no means affected by his internal waverings. The sociologists can provide part of the answer here: 'Even very intelligent people', we are told, 'when faced with doubt about their roles in society, involve themselves even more in the doubted activity rather than withdraw into reflection . . . The role forms, shapes, patterns both action and actor.'[54] This phenomenon has been very closely analysed by Sartre, in his study of 'bad faith' (*mauvaise foi*) or 'self-deception'. 'Bad faith' consists of the pretence that a course of action is necessary, when in fact it is not. The essence of Bosola's situation is that he allows the moral responsibility for the actions he performs to devolve upon his role—overlooking that he himself, of his own free will, chose that role. The point is made with searing irony when Bosola claims his reward. He cites the authority of Ferdinand; and Ferdinand denies his own authority, denies the legality and justice of the decision that sent his sister to the executioners:

---

[53] C. G. Thayer, 'The Ambiguity of Bosola', *Studies in Philology* iv (1957), 162–71.

[54] Peter L. Berger, *Invitation to Sociology* (Penguin, Harmondsworth, 1966), p. 115.

Ferdinand.	By what authority did'st thou execute
	This bloody sentence?
Bosola.	By yours—
Ferdinand.	Mine? was I her Judge?
	Did any ceremoniall forme of Law,
	Doombe her to not-Being? did a compleat Jury
	Deliver her conviction up i'th Court?
	Where shalt thou find this judgement registerd
	Unlesse in Hell? See: like a bloody foole
	Th'hast forfeyted thy life, and thou shalt die for't.
Bosola.	The Office of Justice is perverted quite
	When one Thiefe hangs another:

                                        (iv. ii. 320–30)

Both deny responsibility for their actions. Ferdinand renounces
his right to authorize murder; Bosola, in a defence that reminds
us of Nuremberg, claims that he was only obeying orders. The
responsibility cannot however be evaded. Bosola states his case:

> And though I loath'd the evill, yet I lov'd
> You that did councell it: and rather sought
> To appeare a true servant, then an honest man.
>   (iv. ii. 357–9)

The reward not being forthcoming, he now sees his error. 'Off
my painted honour!' (iv. ii. 362) refers to the ethic of professionalism that he now discards. Bosola comes to a true appraisal
of his situation:

> What would I doe, were this to doe again?
> I would not change my peace of conscience
> For all the wealth of Europe:
>   (iv. ii. 365–7)

This retrospectively negates, and exposes the error of his conduct.

   That error, bad faith, is thus epitomized by Sartre:

I say that it is also a self-deception if I choose to declare that certain
values are incumbent upon me; I am in contradiction with myself if I
will these values, and at the same time say that they impose themselves
upon me. If anyone says to me, 'And what if I wish to deceive myself?'
I answer, 'There is no reason why you should not, but I declare that

you are doing so, and that the attitude of strict consistency alone is that of good faith'.[55]

The role of 'true servant' is incompatible with 'honest man'. The 'role-playing' attitude to life has met its refutation. It has been an implicit assumption of Bosola's conduct that each one of his roles expresses but does not fully define him. But this one does. A 'true servant' cedes his moral autonomy to his master; but he may then be 'in contradiction with' himself. The underlying reason for this one may guess at. It is not purely economic, in Bosola's case. It is a matter of identity. Sartre, in his classic essay, 'Portrait of the Anti-Semite', remarks: 'by adhering to antisemitism, he is not only adopting an opinion, he is choosing himself as a person. He is choosing the permanence and the impenetrability of rock, the total irresponsibility of the warrior who obeys his leaders—and he has no leaders.'[56] For 'anti-semite', read here 'intelligencer'. Bosola's love of role-playing may be regarded in part as a quest for personal identity. His error is to delegate the responsibility for his acts to his role—a situation nakedly revealed by his shamefaced refusal to face the Duchess in his own garb; and rendered totally absurd by the disintegration of his 'leader' before his eyes.

(iv) We have, then, the position that man must come to terms with his own identity. This is the 'attitude of strict consistency', to be identified with Webster's 'integrity of life'. This value is emphasized by a social outlook which is also typically Webster's. The delegation of moral responsibility to one's superior is always to be condemned, on principle. But this act is doubly condemned by the quality of the superior. As Webster sees it, courts are incurably corrupt. The theme of corruption in high places runs throughout his work; it is a thought best summed up by Antonio, 'And let my Sonne, flie the Courts of Princes' (v. iv. 84). In the two tragedies the minor figure of the Marquis of Pescara, alone among the adult male princes, exhibits common decency. The satiric vein in Webster is strong. Consider our masters, he seems to say: delegate our moral autonomy to *them*?

[55] Sartre, 'Existentialism is a Humanism', in *Existentialism from Dostoevsky to Sartre*, p. 307.

[56] Sartre, 'Portrait of the Anti-Semite', in *Existentialism from Dostoevsky to Sartre*, p. 286.

Bosola, then, finds himself physically and morally bankrupt. His solution is the existentialist one : he must choose a course that is consistent with himself, he must define himself in act. But he does not make his commitment immediately. His first decision, after the departure of the demented Ferdinand, is to post to Milan, 'Where somewhat I will speedily enact/Worth my dejection' (IV. ii. 402–3). This is vague. At Milan, following the death of Julia, he decides to help Antonio, perhaps even to league with him : 'It may be,/I'll joyne with thee, in a most just revenge' (V. ii. 377–8). Even yet his resolve is not hardened. The crucial event is the blind scuffle in which he deals Antonio his death wound. Here, at last, Bosola recognizes the 'primary absurdity' of the universe :

> *Antonio?*
> The man I would have sav'de 'bove mine own life!
> We are meerely the Starres tennys-balls (strooke, and banded
> Which way please them)
> —(v. iv. 61–4)

It clinches the matter. Bosola's course is now clear before him; and into this spiritual crisis falls neatly, conclusively, his great existentialist pronouncement :

> Oh, my fate moves swift.
> I have this Cardinall in the forge already,
> Now I'll bring him to th' hammer : (O direfull misprision :)
> I will not Imitate things glorious,
> No more then base : I'll be mine own example.
> (v. iv. 91–5)

The reference to 'fate' is illusive here; it means no more than the current of his life. The individual is asserting himself *against* external events. Bosola, at last, has totally abjured all external authorities, both moral and social ('things glorious'). And perhaps the repudiation of 'Imitate' is also a repudiation of acting. The life-value, found in himself alone, expresses itself in commitment to a 'just cause', and action.

'Action' it becomes : the word is on Bosola's lips as he enters on the last passage of his life :

> Thus it lightens into Action :
> I am come to kill thee.
> (v. v. 11–12)

And this last mission, too, is accomplished. Bosola does not fail
in his assignments. His last words express the philosophy which
he has grown into, and which must represent the conceptual core
of *The Duchess of Malfi*. Bosola's dying speech, after the 'play'
image, makes two points which correspond to the two parts of
our analysis of the knowledge theme:

> (1) We are onely like dead wals, or vaulted graves,
>   That ruin'd, yeildes no eccho: Fare you well—
>
> (v. v. 121–2)

This is the climactic statement of knowledge. It asserts with
finality the unknowability of the void; it negates a Christian or
any other afterlife.

> (2) It may be paine: but no harme to me to die,
>   In so good a quarrell: Oh this gloomy world,
>   In what a shadow, or deepe pit of darknesse,
>   Doth (womanish, and fearefull) mankind live!
>   Let worthy mindes nere stagger in distrust
>   To suffer death, or shame, for what is just—
>   Mine is another voyage.
>
> (v. v. 123–9)

The conclusion Bosola draws is not a philosophy of quietism, it
is a philosophy of action. He not only makes the point, 'so good
a quarrell', he returns to it: 'To suffer death, or shame, for what
is just'. Justice is recognized, confirmed, and asserted by the
individual. And his final duty, consonant with his 'integrity of
life', is to *act*.

(c) *The Duchess*

This interpretation of Bosola, and of the issues he represents,
essentially concludes my analysis of *The Duchess of Malfi*. However, the concluding stages of the Duchess's ordeal do offer the
possibility of an existentialist interpretation, and I shall briefly
consider the passage. The matter becomes philosophically interesting at the point when Bosola, in Act IV, enters dressed as a
tombmaker. The Duchess questions him:

Duchess.	Thou art not mad sure, do'st know me?
Bosola.	Yes.
Duchess.	Who am I?

(IV. ii. 121–2)

The most fundamental question possible—and Bosola answers her in the words already quoted, asserting the twin facts of our mortality and lack of knowledge. 'Am not I, thy Duchesse?' she wonders: Bosola delivers a brief lecture on her premature age: she then makes her statement of the life-value:

I am Duchesse of *Malfy* still.

(IV. ii. 139)

This is a difficult pronouncement. It is certainly more than the theatrical *coup* for which it has been acclaimed. But what exactly does it mean? The Duchess's situation, on both a literal and symbolic level, is that she is in prison. The facts of her literal situation are paralleled by several verbal images of imprisonment of which the most important is 'the Heaven ore our heades, like her looking glasse, onely gives us a miserable knowledge of the small compasse of our prison.' (Apparently, 'The body is the prison of the soul' was a common proverb.[57]) From this passage we derived the philosophy of action. But how can it be applied here? The Duchess, a passive victim of the execution, does not have Bosola's freedom of action. Moreover, if action is hardly possible, what remains of essence? The appurtenances of the Duchy—rank, security, power—have all been stripped from her. As Boklund remarks, 'Webster has methodically taken away all the exterior supports on which she may conceivably have relied to fortify her endurance. From now on she is all alone in a closed room, with nothing outside herself to aid her.'[58] In what does 'Duchesshood' consist, when the recognizable aspects have been removed?

The answer is that action is possible. She can die *like* a Duchess: she can define herself as an identity by behaving at the last as a Duchess should. Several arguments support this view, the parallels with other characters aside. First, 'nobility' as a quality which must be revealed in behaviour not birth is a recurring Websterian theme. Scorn for mere birth, for example, is the substance of the Bosola-Duchess dialogue of III. ii, and is central to *The Devil's Law-Case*. The Arragonian brothers, with their crazed emphasis on their 'blood', are philosophically as well as morally opposed to the Duchess; for them, essence precedes behaviour.

[57] Brown, *The Duchess of Malfi*, p. 123.
[58] Gunnar Boklund, *The Duchess of Malfi: Sources, Themes, Characters* (Harvard University Press, Cambridge, Mass., 1962), p. 113.

Second, the Duchess, like Bosola, utters an actor's image in her
ordeal:

> I account this world a tedious Theatre,
> For I doe play a part in't 'gainst my will.
>
> (IV. i. 99–100)

Her mind is running on tragedies: she wishes one to be read to
her (IV. ii. 9), and speaks of her own tragedy (IV. ii. 38).
Clearly, the Duchess sees herself as playing out a public role. It
is not much; it is indeed highly distasteful; but what else is there
to do? How else can she realize herself at the last?

We seem, therefore, to have the situation and the view of the
situation as expounded in Sartre's *Huis-clos*, when Inez says to
Garcia, 'You are no more than the sum of your acts.' On this
Guicharnaud comments: 'The traditional idea that man commits
such or such act because he is thus and so, is replaced by its
opposite; by committing such or such act, man makes himself
thus and so . . .'[59] Here, as elsewhere, we must not press too
hard an explication on a text for which it was never designed. But
it is a suggestive gloss. For the Duchess, mastering her mental
agony, dies well. She proclaims a public confidence in Heaven
which is completely at variance with her earlier doubts; she
makes the proper orders for the disposal of her children, and of
her own body; she displays great courage and control. It is an
almost faultless performance. The Duchess has answered her own
question, 'Who am I?' in the only possible way; she has defined
herself, as Duchess, in action.

We can now draw together the threads of this analysis of the
knowledge theme. Taken together, they amount to a demonstration of the 'timeless sensibility' to which Kaufmann alluded. In
the most general sense, these ideas are a universe without God,
the 'absurdity' of man's relations with that universe, and the acceptance of death as the human situation together with the necessity it enforces of defining oneself through the mode of dying.
From this Webster derives a philosophy of commitment and
action that is expressed very powerfully through Bosola and the
Duchess:

---

[59] Guicharnaud, 'Man and his Acts', *Sartre*, p. 65.

I'll be mine owne example.
I am Duchesse of *Malfy* still.

It is the same philosophy that is promulgated elsewhere through
Lodovico, Flamineo, and Romelio. In each case, as I have shown,
these sayings may be regarded not merely as cries of individu-
alism—that is sufficiently obvious—but as manifestos for action.
And in the most elaborate of these characterizations, Bosola,
through a series of role-playing actions, comes finally to abjure
those acts which, through 'bad faith', do not express him, and
commits himself to a course of conduct which, whatever its
dangers, does. In this act he dies relatively content: 'It may be
paine:but no harme to me to die,/In so good a quarrell.' All this
bears a considerable resemblance to the beliefs and dramatic
situations propounded by some of our leading existentialist
writers; and with one of them, J.-P. Sartre, I leave the last word,
which may stand as an introduction to much to Webster:

> The doctrine I am presenting before you is precisely the opposite of
> this [quietism], since it declares that there is no reality except in
> action. It goes further, indeed, and adds, 'Man is nothing else but the
> sum of his actions, nothing else but what his life is'.[60]

4. CONCLUSION

A final statement of the themes of *The Duchess of Malfi* and their
interactions, as I interpret them, is now in order. The play depicts man as prone to evil and error, but the state of evil is
apprehended imaginatively not theologically. Man's errors are
embodied in a series of *peripeteias* which attain a philosophical
status, the concept of an 'absurd' universe. Irony is elevated to
a philosophy. This 'absurd' universe derives its meaninglessness
from the absence of God. Hence, the Law metaphor does not rest
on the concept of a 'Divine Law', but exists as a figure for the
mechanisms of action and reaction whereby the universe corrects
man's errors. In this situation, man must generate his own values
and from these decide on his course of action. This, for Bosola, is
commitment to a cause. What emerges from his dying reference
to a 'just' cause is not justice, but rather the choice of a cause felt

[60] Sartre, 'Existentialism is a Humanism', *Existentialism from Dostoevsky to
Sartre*, p. 291.

to be just. (This is quite different from the hope, at least, of 'justice' which Giovanni held out at the end of *The White Devil.*) Bosola's final words, confirmed by Delio, are the reduction of the play's ideas. They express the position on which *The Duchess of Malfi* rests.

IV

THE DEVIL'S LAW-CASE

The Devil's Law-Case has had an attenuated, as much as a bad, press.[61] That neglect probably reflects a critical view of the genre as much as the specific play, and it is worth while separating them here. The critics have always considered tragedy to be the highest kind of drama. For example, much more has been written about Shakespeare's tragedies than his comedies. But the same ratio emerges if one compares comedy to tragicomedy. I know of only one or two modern works devoted to Renaissance tragicomedy. The genre is universally despised. Although Shakespeare wrote tragicomedies, tragicomedy is generally regarded as the mode of Fletcher, hence the genre of some plays not at all to contemporary taste. It is not my purpose here to overturn this very reasonable judgement. Still, a case of sorts can be made

[61] Lucas grants it some fourteen pages of editorial introduction: Lucas, ii. 213–28. There are a few scattered pages of comment, though nothing systematic, in Brooke, op. cit., pp. 102–14; Ellis-Fermor, op. cit., pp. 181–4; and Leech, *John Webster, passim*. T. B. Tomlinson, in *A Study of Elizabethan and Jacobean Tragedy* (C.U.P., Cambridge, 1964), devotes a few pages to it (224–9). His views are necessarily to be treated with some reserve, however, since he follows Bentley in dating the play before the tragedies, a judgement scarcely tenable in the face of Dent's additional evidence for a post-1616 date of composition. This until recently was virtually the sum of contemporary criticism in English; and one can scarcely blame Don D. Moore for the decision, in his survey of Webster criticism, to relegate *The Devil's Law-Case* to a single footnote. (Moore, op. cit., p. 169 note 3). However, much fuller treatment of the play has been available in German and Italian. Ingeborg Glier's careful analysis of the structural techniques employed in the play is in itself a sufficient rejoinder to those who regard Webster as a 'ramshackle' playwright: *Struktur und Gestaltungsprinzipien in den Dramen John Websters* (Munich, 1957), pp. 46–54. This, together with Gabriele Baldini's sympathetic and perceptive account (Baldini, op. cit., pp. 175–210) does much to restore the balance of Anglo-American neglect. Lately there have been signs of a revival of interest in the play. D. C. Gunby, in '*The Devil's Law-Case*: An Interpretation', *Modern Language Review*, lxiii (1968), 545–58, concludes that it is 'Clearly conceived as a thesis play and provided with a didactically directed plot and characters . . .' And Gunnar Boklund, in '*The Devil's Law-Case*—An End or a Beginning?' *John Webster*, ed. Brian Morris (Ernest Benn, London, 1970), suggests: 'It is possible to make a case for *The Devil's Law-Case* as the natural concluding statement of John Webster in the sequence of unpleasant plays which began with *The White Devil*' (p. 129).

out for tragicomedy, and we ought to rehearse it before proceeding to *The Devil's Law-Case*.

Tragicomedy takes to a seemingly logical conclusion the baroque system of mixed elements. It does no more than intensify the tragic element in most, if not all, comedies. (*Much Ado About Nothing* and *The Merchant of Venice*, say, are in effect if not name excellent specimens of the genre.) Tragicomedy is perhaps the most overtly sensationalist of all dramatic forms. It seeks to manipulate the emotions in a sense that goes beyond the normal manipulation of the playwright, since it relies above all on a reversal of expectations. It postulates a virtuoso performance, on the playwright's part, in emotional brinkmanship. It will not deliver what it appears to promise. But this is not dishonest, since the reversals—the fact that the play will not fulfil its apparent predictions—are in the contract. The contract is, that no contracts in the play will be honoured.

Such drama normally leans far more heavily on the mechanisms of plot than on organic development of character interaction. It is the ancestor of such modern formula-writing as the thriller. Still, there is more to tragicomedy than ingenuity of plotting. The form should command attention if only because of the contemporary tendency to synthesize and juxtapose antagonistic modes of feeling in serious drama. Comic-sad is nowadays a common enough juxtaposition; we accept it of mood, but tend puritanically to reject it of plot. And we can distinguish between ingenuities of action that are no more than ends in themselves, and those which embody some coherent principle. The surprise by which Arbaces (in *A King and No King*) turns out not to be the brother of Panthea is a pure surprise, one moreover that makes a nonsense of the issue of Incest Contemplated. But the Capuchin's exclamation at the crisis of *The Devil's Law-Case*

> to see how heaven
> Can invert mans firmest purpose!
>
> (v.iv. 214–15)

reveals Webster identifying the theory underlying his tragedies. The point is a reworking of Bosola's reference to the 'Starres tennys-balls'. The parallelism of the method is emphasized by Fräulein Glier: 'Stärker noch als in DM arbeitet Webster hier mit dem Zufall, dessen Anwendung in der Tragikomödie zur

Methode, zum Strukturprinzip wird, das jede tragische Ver-
wicklung überraschend und—darin besteht der Unterschied zur
Anwendung in der Tragödie—glücklich löst.'[62] Whatever one's
opinion of the accumulation of surprises usually found in tragicomedy, one has to concede that Webster advances here a legitimate theoretical justification of the process.

Within the tragicomedy genre, which has several subspecies,
The Devil's Law-Case can best be regarded as a satiric comedy.
Its principals move in a very clearly defined social milieu, a
milieu which—thinly disguised as Naples—is Jacobean England.
Romelio, Leonora, Contarino, and the rest are representatives
of a society whose struggle for money and social status is observed with a bleak and unforgiving eye, an eye reminiscent of
Jonson's or Middleton's. The gross transgressions of the principals bring them to the brink of tragedy, whence chance plucks
them back. Hence, the theme of the play is law (in its several
aspects) broken. It is a *drame à thèse* which the title clearly announces. Within this dramatic thesis are developed certain
character-studies of a disturbingly three-dimensional quality,
notably Romelio and Leonora. Their personalities are so realis-
tically developed that one is bound to experience the conclusion
as the curtailment of an action concerning which many questions
remain unresolved. To this extent, it may perhaps be conceded
that Webster has not wholly succeeded in his enterprise, which
is to place these realistic portrait-studies in a context better
adapted to the presentation of the typical. Still, the existence of an
ambiguity, a certain undischarged tension, at the final curtain is
no infallible criterion of blame.

An analysis of *The Devil's Law-Case* calls for a method different from that appropriate to the tragedies. *The White Devil* and
The Duchess of Malfi must be studied through their densely packed
metaphors. But *The Devil's Law-Case* has many fewer metaphors.
Moreover, a study based on metaphor would miss the mark; for
the concern of this play is, quite simply, its literal content. Virtually every page contains some literal reference to the Law; only
in the context of the whole play does one observe that these law
references have a collective, symbolic status. Similarly, the many
references to 'devil', 'unnaturall', 'foul' all indicate quite straight-
forwardly the concept of evil. There is no hidden pattern of

[62] Glier, op. cit., p. 48.

imagery to elicit; the play's metaphors tend to develop the
theme perfectly apparent in the manifest content. Accordingly, I
shall confine myself to a fairly brief commentary on the play, in
which I indicate the cruces of the law-evil opposition. I should add
that for this play (especially) it is more than convenient to have
a summary of the plot available. The reader will find one in
Lucas, ii. 222–4, and in Marvin T. Herrick's *Tragicomedy*, pp.
281–2.[63]

1. COMMENTARY

Act I

The opening act sets before us the theme of the infringement of
the natural law; that is, the decent ordering of relationships
among kin. Romelio has scarcely announced his wealth, Barabas-
like, when he reveals his design to marry his sister against her
wishes to Ercole. It is Contarino she loves; Romelio's promise to
Contarino is solely to gull him. 'I will breake the alliance' (I. i.
36). The viciousness of the unnatural Ercole-Jolenta alliance is
implicit in Romelio's own account of it. Satirically, he feigns to
dwell on the delights of marriage with the nobility:

> I shall be proud
> To live to see my little Nephewes ride
> O'the upper hand of their Uncles; and the Daughters
> Be ranckt by Heraulds at Solemnities
> Before the Mother: all this deriv'd
> From your Nobilitie.
> (I. i. 108–13)

Such relationships affront the natural Law, and Romelio thus
prefigures his own fall.

The major metaphor for evil is gold. Here, as in *The White
Devil* (reward and punishment) and *The Duchess of Malfi* (the
realm corrupted by an evil prince) the theme is established in the
opening lines. There is, indeed, a central ambiguity in Prospero's
initial

You have shewen a world of wealth.
(I. i. 1)

The manifest meaning of the line involves a stress on 'world', so

---

[63] Marvin R. Herrick, *Tragicomedy* (University of Illinois Press, Urbana, Ill.,
1955).

that 'world of' is a hyperbolic extension of *wealth*. But an alternative meaning is implicit in the text, if not the spoken line: 'of wealth' is then an adjectival phrase, qualifying *world*. So a world 'of wealth' is a world in which values are created by money. Not only are marriage alliances fixed by money, the gold metaphor dominates men's minds. 'What a Treasury have I pearch'd!' gloats Contarino of Leonora (i. i. 218): 'Have I any interest in you?' asks Romelio of Jolenta (i. ii. 42): Contarino, seeking for a standard to measure traitors by, remarks that they deserve hanging even more than those that counterfeit money (i. ii. 288–9). The opening of *The Devil's Law-Case* is an acid exposition of a society whose leaders—Romelio, the banker, and Contarino, the noble descendant of 'ancient riches'—agree on one thing, at least; the paramountcy of gold.

It is not, of course, a metaphor new to the Jacobean drama. The thing had been done before, most notably by Jonson, Middleton, and Tourneur. The obvious example is *Volpone* (1606), and *The Devil's Law-Case* alone would demonstrate the justice of Webster's compliment to Jonson in his address to the readers of *The White Devil*. Middleton too had assimilated fully the notion of money as the dominant passion of society. In *A Trick to Catch the Old One* (1605–6), for example, Middleton makes such figures as Lucre, Hoord, and Moneylove execute a dance around the mammon idol. Webster's contribution is to link the metaphor with the operations of the Law, thus providing both satire on lawyers (Contilupo especially) and a grave reminder of the concept for which they stand.

The argument of the first scene, then, is that wealth creates rank, and that both together combine to overbear natural relationships. The consequences are visible in the bitter scene (i. ii) in which Romelio and his mother combine to bring pressure to bear on Jolenta to reject Contarino in favour of Ercole. Both suitors are noble; but Ercole is noble and rich. Romelio's motive is contempt for a decayed nobleman; Leonora's, a passion for Contarino destined, as she thinks, for fruition, and necessitating that Jolenta be firmly headed off. The scene's climax is the formal curse which Leonora calls down on her daughter—for wishing to marry for love. This ignoble passage, perhaps the most savagely drawn in the whole of Webster, is interlarded with references to the Law. There is much talk of 'contract', and of the presence of lawyers. A legal metaphor comes easily to Romelio; he urges Ercole:

> Keep your possession, you have the dore bith'ring,
> That's Livery and Seasin in England;
>
> (I. ii. 145–6)

Webster makes clear his view of arranged marriages through Winifred:

> Plague of these
> Unsanctified Matches; they make us lothe
> The most naturall desire our grandame *Eve* ever left us.
> Force one to marry against their will!—why 'tis
> A more ungodly worke, then inclosing the Commons.
>
> (I. ii. 226–30)

This is a choric comment reminiscent of Cariola's at the end of the first act of *The Duchess of Malfi*. And the seal is set on the matter in the following three-cornered dialogue:

Jolenta.	Reach me the Caskanet, I am studying Sir,
	To take an Inventory of all that's mine.
Contarino.	What to doe with it Lady?
Jolenta.	To make you a Deed of gift.
Contarino.	That's done already; you are all mine.
Winifred.	Yes, but the Devil would faine put in for's share,
	In likenesse of a Separation.
Jolenta.	Oh, sir I am bewitcht.
Contarino.	Ha?
Jolenta.	Most certaine, I am forespoken,
	To be married to another: can you ever thinke
	That I shall ever thrive in't? Am I not then
	bewitcht?

> (I. ii. 246–57)

The imagery states the play's concerns. There is the purely legalistic aspect of law, as emphasized in Jolenta's terminology; this is seen to be the Devil's work; underlying it is the appeal to a different aspect of law, that governing natural conduct. The best comment is Winifred's:

> get you instantly to bed together—
> Doe, and I thinke no Civill Lawyer for his fee
> Can give you better Councell.
>
> (I. ii. 299–301)

Act II

The second act introduces us to the civil law, in the shape of the lawyers themselves. The dialogue between Crispiano and Sanitonella, a sustained satire on lawyers, culminates in the remarkable passage in which Crispiano eulogizes the Law as a purely personal gratification:

> For neither Wine, nor Lust, nor riotous feasts,
> Rich cloathes, nor all the pleasure that the Devill
> Has ever practis'd with, to raise a man
> To a Devils likenesse, ere brought man that pleasure
> I tooke in getting my wealth: so I conclude.
> If he can out-vie me, let it flie to'th Devill.
>
> (II. i. 88–93)

These two are contrasted with Ariosto, who has a finer concept of the Law than money-making. Ariosto's 'carracter' helps to provide a core of decency to the play, one which saves it from complete cynicism:

Crispiano.	There he stands, but a little piece of flesh,
	But he is the very myracle of a Lawyer,
	One that perswades men to peace, & compounds quarrels
	Among his neighbours, without going to law.
Sanitonella.	And is he a Lawyer?
Crispiano.	Yes, and will give counsell
	In honest causes gratia—never in his life
	Tooke fee, but he came and spake for't —is a man
	Of extreame practise, and yet all his longing
	Is to become a Judge.
Sanitonella.	Indeed that's a rare longing with men of his profession
	I think heel prove the miracle of a lawier indeed.
	(II. i. 107–18)

Hardly is Ariosto introduced when another reversal of the natural law is stated. The disguised Crispiano announces his death to his son Julio, who receives the news with perfect composure, enquiring only whether his father made him heir. Young Julio is thereupon roundly reproached by Ariosto, the man who would be judge. It is already apparent that Ariosto is a symbolic figure of some importance, one who will support the ideal of law.

Following the duel scene, comes the first Romelio-Ariosto dialogue. Here 'honesty' is confronted with Romelio's 'devilishness'. Again, the nature of Romelio's course is heavily underlined:

Ariosto.	You gave those ships most strange, most dreadfull, and
	Unfortunate names—I never lookt they'd prosper.
Romelio.	Is there any ill Omen in giving names to ships?
Ariosto.	Did you not call one, *The Stormes Defiance*;
	Another, *The Scourge of the Sea*; and the third,
	The Great Leviathan?
Romelio.	Very right sir.
Ariosto.	Very devillish names . . . .

(II. iii. 59–65)

Romelio resists him, as he does the Capuchin; his 'meditation' is an echo of earlier themes, a refusal to look beyond the grave. (Characteristically for this play, a legal metaphor—'supersedeas' —is inserted even here, II. iii. 132.) The idea of the Law is maintained before the audience when Leonora desires to keep Ercole alive, 'To come to his tryall, to satisfie the Law' (II. iii. 184). Justice for all appears now the compulsive issue of the play; and one may look for severity in the sentences, for the crimes of the dramatis personae are great. Romelio, who ends II. iii meditating on the evil of riches, is to proceed to murder. And of the guilt he has already incurred, the Capuchin observes:

> These are crimes
> That either must make worke for speedy repentance,
> Or for the Devill.
> (II. iv. 45–7)

Here, as in *The White Devil*, Webster suggests that the laws of cause and effect are not of iron, and that repentance can save a sinner. It is another piece of evidence to weigh against the 'Calvinist' view of Webster's outlook. Ercole, for one, has seen the error of his ways, and formally renounces his interest in Jolenta.

Act III

The third act, after a brief scene stressing the monstrousness of women (a strong hint of the sub-title), reveals Romelio about to commit a crime against the supreme law, wherein he is frustrated purely by chance. The Machiavellian pastiche of III. ii. 1–16 is a satiric rendering of evil, just as Romelio's reference to the 'Law of alliance' (III. ii. 53) is a satiric invocation to good. For the surgeons, those connoisseurs of villainy, the matter is purely an opportunity for blackmail. One cannot but respond to the simple lyricism of the surgeon's vision of the future: 'Ile presently grow a lazy Surgeon, & ride on my foot-cloth; Ile fetch from him every eight dayes a policy for a hundred double Duckets; if hee grumble, Ile peach' (III. ii. 155–7). But however rich the comic vein is hereabouts, the surgeons represent the serious business of the play: the mesh of gold, evil, and corrupted law.

The long scene of III. iii marks a return to the most overt aspects of the evils linked with the Law. The talk is of 'pre-contracts', 'lawyers', 'heirs'; but the real point is Romelio's scheme to flout the natural law. This is, for Jolenta, a 'witching' of her fame, but Romelio clinches the matter with a 'most un-naturall falshood' which the 'Devill' has put into his head (103–4). The falsehood, Leonora's love for Contarino, is in fact true; nevertheless Romelio's 'the malice scarse of Devils would suggest/Incontinence 'tweene them two' is a self-portrait (121–2). The irony is intense, as it is with his advice to Jolenta: 'Throw the fowle to the Devill that hatcht it . . .' (158). Against this background of evil, and twisted law, is set Jolenta's invocation to the divine law:

> I doe call any thing to witnesse,
> That the divine law prescribed us to strengthen
> An oath, were he living and in health, I would never
> Mary with him.
> (III. iii. 171–4)

But Jolenta is ready falsely to give out that she carries Ercole's child; no scandal, since it was a matter of 'precontract'; the satire is acid. The theme then passes from Jolenta to her mother:

> oh Jelousie,
> How violent, especially in women,
> How often has it raisd the devil up
> In forme of a law-case!
> (III. iii. 215–18)

says Romelio, forecasting unconsciously his own fall. For Leonora determines to avenge Contarino's death on her son; it is evil masquerading as justice. The situation itself is not less terrible than the lines that conclude this meeting between mother and son:

> *Leonora, aside*   I am rapt with the Mother indeed,
> That I ever bore such a sonne.
> *Romelio.*   Pray tend my sister,
> I am infinitely full of businesse.
> *Leonora.*   Stay, you will mourne
> For *Contarino?*
> *Romelio.*   Oh by all meanes, tis fit—
> My sister is his heire.
>   (iii. iii. 258–64)

Decidedly, some of the best things in Webster's theatre are to be found in this play. Jonson could not have bettered the five sublime concluding words of Romelio, wherein he reduces all social decency to a factor of gold. And Romelio has a perfect awareness of what he is saying. The creation is Balzacian.

The whole scene is very well carried off by Webster. The despair of Leonora, deprived of her final lover, is that of reality not a formula of fiction:

> Is he gone then?
> There is no plague i'th world can be compared
> To impossible desire, for they are plagued
> In the desire it selfe: never, oh never
> Shall I behold him living, in whose life
> I live farre sweetlier than in mine owne.
>   (iii. iii. 268–73)

With this, and 'I am whispering to a dead friend' (317), Leonora confirms her three-dimensional status in a play that must carry its quota of pasteboard. It is an absolute necessity of stagecraft; the act of malevolence that drives the play through the trial scene must be convincingly underwritten.

Act IV

The fourth act is the play's climax, as each character in turn is subjected to the pressures of the Law. First comes the Ariosto-Contilupo contrast; the former rejects his brief, making a plea for decency in the conduct of the civil law:

Woman, y'are mad, Ile swear't, & have more need
Of a Physician then a lawyer.
  The melancholly humour flowes in your face,
    Your painting cannot hide it: such vild suits
Disgrace our Courts, and these make honest Lawyers
Stop their owne eares, whilst they plead. . . .
Bad Suits, and not the Law, bred the Lawes shame.
(IV. i. 66–71, 77)

This, especially the last line, is at the play's heart. It is a statement of values that gives *The Devil's Law-Case* balance and sanity.
But Contilupo can read the 'foule' copy—an important pun. The
point is hammered in, with the striking-out of 'vivere honeste'
and Sanitonella's

> Oh give me such a Lawyer, as wil think
> Of the day of Judgment!
(IV. i. 126–7)

  Now follows the trial scene. Romelio, that 'subtill Devill',
must endure the charge of bastardy. Here especially Webster's
dramaturgy has received much less than its due. Manifestly the
scene is brilliant theatre. And it is easy to regard its *coups* as
sheer trickery, the product of an approach to drama that is
essentially akin to Fletcher's. But the central situation of the
scene, the man charged with bastardy, has a dramatic validity
that is independent of its immediate theatrical effect. The focus
of the scene is Romelio; he is a totally self-possessed egotist, a
ready parodist of evil and good whose personal self-sufficiency
rests on the foundation of money. Romelio in the first three acts
gives the impression of a man whose role-playing propensities
are based on a profession that he has mastered, banking. But the
charge deprives him of his birth, hence his career base. He is a
nothing, the zero to which all the major Websterian characters
are reduced before they find themselves. Significantly, Contilupo's attack—rubbed in by Ariosto—assesses the gold-man in
financial, not human terms:

> *Contilupo.*   What title shall I set to this base coyne?—
>   He has no name. . . .
>   . . . . I will sell him to any
>   man
> For an hundred Chickeens, and he that buyes him of me,
> Shall loose byth hand too.

Ariosto.   Loe, what you are come to:
                    You that did scorne to trade in any thing,
                    But Gold or Spices, or your Cochineele—
                    He rates you now at poore John.
                                        (IV. ii. 144–55)

The agony of Romelio leads to his outburst against bastardy:

                    Yet why doe I
          Take Bastardy so distastfully, when i'th world,
          A many things that are essentiall parts
          Of greatnesse, are but by-slips, and are father'd
          On the wrong parties?
          Preferment in the world a many times,
          Basely begotten? nay, I have observ'd
          The immaculate Justice of a poore mans cause,
          In such a Court as this, has not knowen whom
          To call Father, which way to direct it selfe
          For Compassion; but I forget my temper—
          Onely that I may stop that Lawyers throat,
          I doe beseech the Court, and the whole world,
          They will not thinke the baselyer of me,
          For the vice of a mother: for that womans sinne,
          To which you all dare sweare when it was done,
          I would not give my consent.
                                        (IV. ii. 340–56)

Romelio himself has fathered a bastard upon Angiolella, and his
final line here has an obvious irony. But the speech is serious,
and meant to be taken seriously. Romelio sees 'bastardy' as the
central metaphor for disorder and wrong in society. Adultery,
and not gold, is the main evil that he can perceive.

The judge, Crispiano, provides an elegiac perspective on the
troubles of Leonora and Romelio. For him, Leonora's charge is
an offence against the natural law, and his reminiscence of
Hooker suggests a framework of past stability for a disordered
society:

                    we observe
          Obedience of creatures to the Law of Nature
          Is the stay of the whole world; here that Law is broke,
          For though our Civill Law makes difference
          Tween the base, and the ligitimate; compassionat Nature
          Makes them equall, nay, shee many times preferres them.
                                        (IV. ii. 275–80)

It is one of the key viewpoints on the action. The machinations of Leonora (and earlier, Romelio) are evil because they are 'unnaturall' (a constantly recurring word); they make use of the civil law to break the law of nature. Here, as in *The Duchess of Malfi* (IV. i. 43) we have a reference to that 'compassionate Nature' whose kindliness stands in contrast to the social world of man.

The supposed offence of Leonora is, however, a breach of something higher than the natural or civil law. It is the concept that Crispiano voices, completing the triad of law levels expressed in the scene:

> How many ills spring from Adultery!
> First, the supreame Law that is violated,
> Nobilitie oft stain'd with Bastardy,
> Inheritance of Land falsly possest,
> The husband scorn'd, wife sham'd and babes unblest.
>
> (IV. ii. 482–6)

Here again, as with Jolenta earlier, is the idea of a higher ('divine' or 'supreme') law governing these acts. It is a statement of values that is in no way modified by the later course of the play.

It is, however, the civil law that now comes into its own, as soon as Crispiano points out that the accusation lacks proof (IV. ii. 358). The examination of Winifred is high comedy that must surely, one day, be added to the classic English repertory. Webster's reputation as a tragedian has obscured his talent for comedy; and the tale of the tennis-court woollen slippers, the julep brought to the bedside of the 'wondrous thirstie' Crispiano, and the young thing drawn arsy-versy into the business, is one that must some day be retold to the delectation of English audiences. It is succeeded by the scene's major *coup de théâtre*, Crispiano's descent from the bench. Symbolically, it is a moment of great importance, for Crispiano delegates his functions to the man of conscience, Ariosto. Ariosto's wishes have at last come true. He is to be judge. In spite of his misgivings

> This Law businesse
> Will leave me so small leasure to serve God,
> I shall serve the King the worse.
>
> (IV. ii. 499–501)

he accepts the charge. Through Crispiano, the facts become known. 'Truth will out in spite of the Devill' comments Winifred (IV. ii. 517). The consequences of the truth affect all and form the matter of the final act. That this is an essential part of Webster's purpose, and not merely an irrelevant extension of the play, we may infer from Julio's groan: 'I could never away from after reckonings' (IV. ii. 566). The utterance is transformed to a comic vein, but fundamentally it is serious. It is in fact the staple of tragedy in the two earlier plays.

Act V

Tragedy, however, is precisely what the fifth act avoids. The Capuchin-Romelio dialogue of V. iv retraces the ground of the earlier plays. The Capuchin takes over Bosola's role as the *agent provocateur* of the condemned. He is fain to 'justle the devill' out of Romelio's way (87); it is reminiscent of Antonio's assessment of Bosola. But Romelio sees the matter in different terms. After the outburst of the trial scene, he reasserts that total self-control which is his commanding characteristic. Indeed, his very metaphor indicates that he has recovered from the trauma of the trial:

> No, no, the world and I
> Have not made up our accounts yet.
>   (V. iv. 53-4)

The metaphors of a Websterian principal *in extremis* have always a terrible exactness, and it must be taken here as a sign that Romelio is reasserting the mode of existence which has been his life base. Further than that, Romelio's intention is simply to hold to that 'honesty' which consists of rejecting cowardice. The passage is a lapidary reduction of some major ideas in the tragedies, notably that of the life-force, 'I doe now/Labour for life, for life!' (62-3) that insists on defining itself: 'I will be mine owne Pilot' (58). Yet this attitude coexists with an elegiac recognition of the impermanence of all earthly things: 'All the Flowers of the Spring/Meet to perfume our burying' (131-2).

The stage is now set for tragedy. The actions of the principals have set up reactions whose resolution seems destined to be bitter. Moreover, these actions occur in an ironic universe which confounds the intentions of the principals. The Capuchin makes the point:

> to see how heaven
> Can invert mans firmest purpose!
>
> (v. iv. 214–15)

It is the most explicit statement Webster ever makes concerning a fundamental aspect of tragedy. For him it is *peripeteia*, which is to say, irony in action. But *peripeteia* is not exclusive to tragedy. It can shower benefits on the undeserving. And this is what occurs in the final two pages of *The Devil's Law-Case*: the fabric of tragedy dissolves, the theme of evil rebuked by the Law melts into an insipid pairing-off, and we are left with a conclusion that appears to invite the least charitable of the epithets that are customarily applied to tragicomedy.

Nevertheless, the conclusion is something more than a homage to Fletcher. The note struck on the final page is not one of authorial tiredness or incapacity. It is Ariosto who dominates the concluding lines; and from him, the honest lawyer, something of Webster's own judgement may perhaps be inferred:

> now it does remaine,
> That these so Comicall events be blasted
> With no severitie of Sentence:
>
> (v. v. 68–70)

It is a grimace, surely; the events seemed hardly so 'comicall' a little earlier. The note is sounded more clearly in Ariosto's final words, which bring down the curtain:

> so we leave you,
> Wishing your future life may make good use
> Of these events, since that these passages,
> Which threatned ruine, built on rotten ground,
> Are with successe beyond our wishes crown'd.
>
> (v. v. 98–102)

Now these are Webster's last words which have survived to us in a play known to be solely his, and I think they should be weighed with the greatest respect. 'Beyond our wishes' is the phrase that lingers. Here is the voice of the frustrated moralist. We have seen a play deeply concerned with the Law in three aspects— divine (or supreme), natural, and civil; and in each aspect the Law has been flouted, a process which Webster consistently presents as the Devil's work. And the concluding punishments meted out are more appropriate than they look. All the dramatis personae—Romelio, Contarino, Leonora, Jolenta, Angiolella, and the two surgeons—are punished *financially*; they have severally to maintain gallies, serve in them, and build a monastery. In view of the central social sin that flaws them all, the denizens of the 'world of wealth' can hardly be said to be unjustly treated. Romelio, too, in view of his outcry against bastards, has to face the highly appropriate atonement of making an honest woman of Angiolella.

Justice is far from absent from the conclusion of *The Devil's Law-Case*.[64] It is not enforced *à l'outrance*, but I do not see this as a major criticism; in the comparable *Measure for Measure* Angelo, like Romelio, is forgiven his major crimes and let off with marriage. But I should prefer to read the ending of *The Devil's Law-Case* as something besides a compromise with justice. It is, in its way, a perfectly apt comment on the values depicted in the play. Moore speaks of the 'crumbling world' of Webster;[65] the conclusion here erects into a formal statement the awareness of a crumbling society. For the society depicted is evidently and explicitly *rotten*. Webster plays on the word (together with 'foul', 'unnaturall', and the occasional disease image) as a means of fixing his apprehension of Neapolitan/Jacobean society. He uses the word 'rotten' precisely as Shaw does in *The Shewing-Up of Blanco Posnet*. A tragedy may make the statement that this is a rotten world; tragicomedy, which in this instance is satiric comedy, can appropriately state that this is a rotten society. And this is what Webster does. The threadbare justice of the concluding lines is felt keenly by one person only, the point of reference of the play. Ariosto has to contemplate a society whose transgressions must be fined rather than punished. His very curtain-line is no cadence of resolution, but a dissonance that stays vibrating in the mind.

> these passages,
> Which threatned ruine, built on rotten ground,
> Are with successe beyond our wishes crown'd.

[64] I suspect that this is precisely what Webster is alluding to in his prefatory address: 'A great part of the grace of this (I confess) lay in Action.' The action, much more than the text, can convey the principals' sour awareness that they have not been let off scot-free. Romelio's final 'Most willingly', for example, demands to be spoken hollowly.

[65] Moore, op. cit., p. 162.

The last words of *The Devil's Law-Case* are spoken by an impotent judge. May we not consider such a figure to possess symbolic value?

CONCLUSION

It is hard to disagree with Signor Baldini's verdict on *The Devil's Law-Case*: 'la principale caratteristica del *Devil's Law-Case* sia nel fatto che l'interesse per la macchina dell'intreccio soffoca e (nel caso di Romelio) compromette un più autentico interesse drammatico, così come le risonanze più intime delle voci dei personaggi.'[66] I think Signor Baldini has correctly identified the price Webster paid for this original and disturbing dramatic creation—the intrigue, the unresolved resonances of the characters are nonetheless a necessary part of Webster's fable. We can now describe this fable, while relating it to Webster's past work.

Webster is obsessed with the idea of law and contract, reward and punishment. It haunts each of his plays. He is a moralist fascinated with the problem of calibrating punishment to offence. Now the essence of Fletcherian tragicomedy is that no contracts are honoured, that human beings are spared the consequences of their own actions. It is totally opposed to Webster's vision. Such a man must regard Fletcherian tragicomedy with contempt, for the form negates his whole system of values. Temperamentally, Webster is of Jonson's stamp. One would expect, then, that a tragicomedy by Webster would end on lines similar to *Volpone*, with appropriately brutal punishment meted out to all the malefactors. What one finds is an ending that appears to copy Fletcher, but actually grimaces at him. The final page of *The Devil's Law-Case* is a cross between Jonson and Fletcher, the cry of a playwright whose total contempt for the values of the society in which he finds himself is manifest not in his whip, but in the sneer with which he lays the whip aside.

The Devil's Law-Case is above all an analysis of social evil, one that follows logically upon the two tragic analyses of human evil. Evil here is related to gold, the mainspring of social wrong. The Law in all its aspects confronts, but can at the end only rebuke this evil. It expresses an *indignatio* none the less *saeva* for being suppressed.

[66] Baldini, op. cit., pp. 208–9.

V

CONCLUSION

THE critical problem that Webster presents is still exacting. No playwright has borrowed more widely and more identifiably from the phrases of his contemporaries, yet the picture of a mere industrious magpie dissolves when one considers the evidence of assimilation and transmutation that R. W. Dent has assembled. None of his fellows has acknowledged more forthrightly and generously the debt to his colleagues, yet the 'personality' of the dramatist Webster is, perhaps, easier to detect than any other. All agree that Webster was a very great original. Yet many have held that his craftsmanship is a mere rickety scaffolding on which a succession of great theatrical moments can be mounted, and that there is no true substance to his most ambitious plays.

The conclusion of this study is that such a view is untenable. I have argued that his techniques can be usefully approached as an early example of baroque. Baroque validates the major characteristics of Webster's work—its dynamic, emotive, and theatrical nature. The term readily extends to cover the multiplex irony of Webster: the ironies of past/future, appearance/reality, parody and caricature. It comprehends his absorption in the contradictions and indefinable elements of human psychology. And it accords well with the subordination of the part to the whole, the organic interconnections of action, character, and imagery that characterize his work. Baroque principles account for the leading techniques of a Webster play, and his execution of them is a triumph of cunningly wrought artistry.

The substance of his plays dispels the charge of moral vacuity. Each play displays a profound apprehension of evil, and projects numerous mutations on this theme. Each play, in turn, hinges on the central concept of the Law—the moralist's metaphor, whereby every manifestation of evil is tested and rebuked by the sanctions of time. The Law implies a variety of aspects—the moral, civil, and natural correctives of human conduct, or the retributive reactions of life itself—but its opposition to natural evil is at the heart of his work. The triptych of trial scenes in his plays properly symbolizes Webster's major preoccupation, and the claims that must be advanced for him as a serious dramatist.

His place among his colleagues Webster has very considerably chosen for himself. The reaction of a modern reader to Webster's address to the readers of *The White Devil* is almost bound to be, at first, one of scepticism:

For mine owne part I have ever truly cherisht my good opinion of other mens worthy Labours, especially of that full and haightned stile of Maister Chapman: The labor'd and understanding workes of Maister Johnson: The no lesse worthy composures of the both worthily excellent Maister Beamont, & Maister Fletcher: And lastly (without wrong last to be named) the right happy and copious industry of M. Shake-speare, M. Decker, & M. Heywood, wishing what I write may read by their light.

Surely, one wonders, the collocation of Shakespeare with two prolific hacks cannot be taken seriously? Surely the 'right happy and copious industry' is a detectable sneer from a notoriously slow worker? And then, perhaps, one begins to overreact in the direction of Swinburne, seeing Webster as sitting at Shakespeare's right hand and therefore greatly under his influence; and then one tends to follow Mr. Bogard in his counterreaction, rightly stressing Webster's explicit debt to Jonson and Chapman but underplaying the role of Shakespeare. But—mere verbal borrowing apart—*The Duchess of Malfi* could not have been written without *King Lear*; and yet the gulf in temperament and aptitude between Shakespeare and Webster is immense. So in the end one comes back to the realization that Webster, quite simply, means what he says. He reserves the address, '*maître*', for Chapman and Jonson; he politely acknowledges the two most successful dramatists of the day, Beaumont and Fletcher; he handsomely brackets two old friends and collaborators with Shakespeare, which as he well knows is more honour to them than Shakespeare. The impression that one is left with, of Webster's debt to other men's labours, is scarcely at variance with his own statement of the matter. Nor are the omissions startling. To extend the list, as Webster legitimately could, to Middleton, Marston, the shadowy Tourneur, and others, would incur the risk of depriving the acknowledgement of all meaning by sketching in a playwright's *Who's Who* of 1612. The contours of his genealogy need not be in doubt, any more than the spirit with which Webster acknowledges his peers; it is of a piece with the surly integrity that breathes from all his prefaces. The vivid fusion of debt and originality is still the central paradox of Webster.

INDEX